How To Get
The Ultimate Guide

Get the girl you've been looking for your whole life - With contributions from over 2,000 girls

3rd Edition

Chad Scott

www.ChadScottCoaching.com

Includes 2 Free Bonuses

90 Min. Confidence Training Video

Plus... Choose 1 Free Book

Redemption Instructions at end of book

Introduction – Max Capacity

I would imagine you're anxious to jump in and get started but before you dive in prematurely (pun intended), I'd like to give you some necessary background info and a jolt of motivation so you actually go the distance.

First off, if you're not already familiar with my books or trainings you may be wondering, who the hell am I and how am I qualified to teach this stuff.

I'm a relationship coach, entrepreneur, musician, adrenaline addict and adventurer of oceans and mountains.

Ever since I was a little kid, I've been incredibly curious why people act the way they do, constantly questioning, studying and seeking answers to life's most puzzling riddles.

Of course, women are indeed one of those big riddles and just like most guys out there, I've had plenty of blank moments, broken hearts and rejection along my journey to find the right one.

In my 20's and 30's, I found myself as the guy who would've normally gotten the gal he always wanted but lost her to some less qualified guy, which drove me fiercely towards solving the riddle of women. The first thing I realized in my journey was this:

Not all women will be your type, no matter how qualified you are!

Personally, I struggled in and out of relationships for 15 years and ended up in some really painful ones that siphoned off several years of my life.

Fortunately, this pain, as all pain does, held within it, an opportunity, which led me to get certified as a relationship coach at the Christopher Howard Leadership Academy and study from many of the greatest relationships experts in the world like Dr. John Gottman, Tony Robbins, and David Deida amongst others.

My relationship challenges also pushed me to study from many of the so-called "PUA gurus" (pick up artists) out there, who claim they can pick up just about any gal and have sex with them in one night.

Interestingly, what I found was that a lot of this PUA stuff is just cheesy, recycled hype and will get you rejected in a heartbeat. In the same token, I have to admit, some of it works incredibly well.

So I'm going to help you filter through the good, the bad and the ugly, and by the end of the book, you'll know what really works and what doesn't.

The Plight Of Man

While my particular situation may be different from yours, as men, we all share the same plight.

First, we must understand women in order to attract them.

Second, we must satisfy them to keep them committed.

And third, we must learn how to become a team member and win at the game of relationships.

While your goal may be to find a great girlfriend, the tools and strategies in this book function to create a much larger goal, namely, the maximization of your capacity.

I once heard the following quote from a mentor of mine:

**Your goal in life is to
maximize your capacity!**

But what is "Maximizing Capacity" and why is it important?

Capacity, according to Webster's dictionary is defined as follows:

"Your ability or power to do, experience, or understand something."

This not only includes attracting and finding the girl of your dreams but making money, solving problems and becoming healthy, strong, personable and immensely confident.

But why maximize capacity, it just sounds like a lot of work?

This brings us back to the reason you most likely bought this book because expanding your capacity will attract women… in herds!

Not only that but maximizing your capacity feels freaking amazing. It's like breaking out of a prison you've been trying to get out of your whole life; you'll be free to do whatever you want because fear doesn't hold you back. Problems and barriers become non-existent because your capacity now exceeds the size of the problems.

When you get to this point, walking up to a beautiful girl and introducing yourself will be like walking up to a cashier at a grocery store, you won't even think twice.

While we can't all become the Michael Jordan of basketball or the Steve Jobs of computers, the good news is, we all have the potential to increase this capacity in various areas of life.

Just keep in mind, it doesn't happen overnight and it requires that we learn new distinctions and overcome some personal limitations.

The Graveyard of Broken Dreams

Let's face it, just rolling with the status quo, doing only what is expected of you will never push you to your limits.

As an unfortunate result of this common pitfall, most people are just comfortable, getting by but not really living exciting lives, breaking through limitations and seeing what they are really made of.

They never end up with the girl they really wanted or go on the vacations they dreamed about and usually have lots of regrets at the end of life, not to mention a life threatening disease.

I like to call this place "The Graveyard of Broken Dreams."

Unfortunately, there's a huge price to pay for not maximizing your capacity, as documented by former palliative care nurse Bronnie Ware in her book, "The Top Five Regrets of the Dying." Can you guess what the #1 regret at the end of life was?

"The #1 regret at the end of life is not having the courage to live a life true to oneself but rather, doing what was expected."

In other words, by giving up on your dreams and doing what everybody else expects you to do, at the end of your life, chances are, you'll feel loads of regrets and depression.

Fortunately, this book will show you simple ways to get out of your comfort zone and expand not only your opportunities with women but also your opportunities in life.

How To Use This Book

To get the most out of this book, make sure you read it from start to finish and try not to skip around on the first read. The first 3 chapters are about understanding girls, getting clear about what you want and how to attract them. These three chapters will be applied to all of the remaining chapters, so make sure you get clear on those before you move on to chapters 4 - 12.

Female Contributions

Throughout this book, you will see contributions from girls I polled on Facebook and in person. Pay close attention to these, as they come straight from the source and will give you insight into what girls are really thinking.

Although I polled over 2,000 girls, I've narrowed down the contributions to represent the voice of the majority and sprinkled them in for greater insight.

Turn Off Distractions

Now hopefully all this talk of thousands of girls, life expansion and superhero stuff has you excited and you're ready to read every word of this book. So go ahead and turn off all distractions and buckle down.

The simple act of focusing on one thing and turning off your phone will give you the first big advantage you'll need if you are to break through your own limitations, maximize your capacity and attract not only lots of beautiful girls but more importantly, the girl you've been looking for your whole life.

Let's dive in!

Chapter 1 - Unlocking the Mystery of Women

Over the course of your dating adventures, chances are you've experienced at least one if not hundreds of perplexing if not completely irrational behaviors from women. These behaviors may have left you frustrated, alone, rejected and yearning for some understanding; so one of the first things we'll do is dispel some of this bewilderment with some basic and not so basic truths.

> *"When I want him to talk to me, sometimes he just bails out and I don't see him for a couple days. Why do guys do this?" - Krisinda*

From a psychological and biological perspective, women are indeed quite different than men.

While we're both from the same human species, girls can sometimes behave so differently that you might as well as assume they're from another planet. Perhaps you even read the book, which highlighted this anomaly "Men are from Mars and Women are from Venus?"

While it's not all true or factual, the book makes a few great points as to the disparity between men and women.

There are indeed some obvious biological differences in men and women, like our sexual features and reproductive organs but the not so obvious is the unseen elements, like oxytocin, a chemical produced in our bodies.

This is significant since oxytocin is much more pronounced in women, especially after giving birth, which makes them love a baby even if the baby looks like an oversized rat. It also makes girls want to stay close and cuddle after sex, while men could go to sleep the moment after orgasm or completely abandon a woman and their offspring.

Are All Girls Crazy?

Some of the things girls do may seem totally illogical to a man but only a few are really crazy. There is no getting away from this fact, so first realize that some of the strategies in this book may seem counterintuitive but... THEY WORK!

On the other hand, be aware of the crazy ones. These are the ones that stalk you, read your email, are super jealous, demand all your time and have extreme mood changes from really happy to really sad.

While we humans want to treat everyone equally and show compassion, if you encounter a girl who fits this description, you may, in fact, be dealing with someone who is suffering from major mental instability and desperately in need of therapy or medication. ,

Believe me, I've been there and if you don't draw the line and demand change, they will literally drag you down into a living hell.

Men Want Sex - Women Want Love, Romance & Security

One of the most striking differences in men and women is what attracts them. In my personal experience and from polling women, depending on age, the three main things most women want are love, romance and security.

According to Dr. Helen Fisher of Rutgers University, men are attracted to women who possess "youth and beauty" and would make good sex partners, while women look for security in the way of "money, status and ambition" so they and their offspring can be taken care of.

The only problem here is that security or money, in particular, is a double-edged sword. Yes, having money will help her feel that you can bring security to her life but in the beginning of a relationship, it's important NOT to buy everything and woo her with money. This communicates: "Sorry this is all I have to offer" and sets you up as just the provider.

Fortunately, the good news is that security and money only provide a "feeling", which you can create through other attraction factors.

Use Your Best Bait

My favorite analogy for attracting women is that of the fisherman. To catch the best fish, the fisherman takes some time and effort to figure out what the most irresistible bait would be.

For example, when he fishes in the river he'll use different bait than when he's fishing in the deep sea.

Similarly, you'll need to think about different bait for different situations. So remember, in order to hook her at the beginning, you'll want to rely more on your personality for bait than your wallet.

According to Roland Warren of the National Fatherhood Initiative, good fathers, do three things:

1) Provide
2) Nurture
3) Guide

Problem is, most men misinterpret "providing" to be strictly the provider of gifts and monetary support when in actuality what's more important is their "presence" or just being there.

This provider concept is not only important in fathering but in dating as well, as you'll soon discover, providing is opposite the lover and instead of building attraction will put you quite quickly in a woman's "friend" zone.

Attraction Doesn't Always Lead to Compatibility

If you're not over 6 feet tall, tan, muscular and possess a perfectly sculpted jawline, don't worry. While there are exceptions, most women are not like most men whose main qualifier is looks. Women are more interested in how you make them feel.

Women are more interested in how you make them feel

That being said, I can tell you first hand, girls are indeed attracted to "tall dark and handsome," so here's **a huge tip** that you'll never get from some dating guru that never got any dates growing up.

As a decent looking guy with a lot going for me, I've had women look at me all my life, but just being handsome NEVER attracted my ideal match.

Similarly, "Famous" or "Wealthy" are two other instant attractors for most girls, but again they almost NEVER lead to an ideal match.

Just think about all the celebrity breakups, like Brad Pit and Jennifer Aniston, Brad Pitt and Angelina Jolie, Tom Cruise and Katie Holmes, Heidi Klum and Seal, Arnold Schwarzenegger and Maria Shriver, Tiger Woods and Elin Nordegren. Need I go on? If these people were so happy and attractive why do they go through breakup after breakup and experience so much pain?

"Come to think of it, my last three relationships all started with intense attraction, lots of sex, but within 6 months they were over and ended badly." - Beth

So why don't handsome, wealthy or famous guarantee relationship success? While these all build immense and instant attraction,

attraction by itself is a poor indicator of compatibility.

"Attraction" is a poor indicator of compatibility!

The problem here relates to incompatible values and beliefs. Being famous, good looking or wealthy will always be overridden and negated if you have two totally different belief systems.

Remember, girls are more interested in how you make them feel. What's most important to understand here is the "FEELING" from handsome and famous can be duplicated by other means (more on this shortly).

Practice What You Can't Do

Something I heard a long time ago by the millionaire solon products magnate Paul Mitchell really resonated with me. It went something like this:

"Work hard at the things most people don't want to do and you'll get whatever you want."

This is what maximizes capacity and separates Tiger Woods from all the other pro golfers, Michael Jordan from all the other basketball players and what will make you a master at attracting, interacting and finding that ideal match.

In other words, when it comes to girls, what are you bad at that you avoid because it's TOO

Difficult? Probably approaching girls, or speaking to them I'd imagine.

Well, if you'd like to expand your capacity so you don't think twice about approaching or speaking to a woman, you'll need to make a commitment to yourself to actually apply these strategies I teach, as they will only help you if you take action and get good at them.

Some of it is simple and will change the reaction you get from women overnight and some may take a full year of practice. Regardless of how long it takes to get good, make a commitment that from here on out you simply won't give up practicing until you get the result you want - your ideal match.

Chapter 2 - What Is Chemistry & Can I Get More?

Ok so we know girls are different from men and it's important to take these things into consideration during all phases of a relationship but what about Chemistry? Do you have to have it in order to be attracted and can it be created if you don't have it with someone?

We've all heard the phrase: "We just don't have any chemistry," which is referred to quite a bit amongst the dating elite, so let's check out Wikipedia's definition which, to me feels most accurate:

"Chemistry can be described as a combination of love, lust, infatuation, and a desire to be involved intimately with someone. It contains the components of non-judgment, similarity, mystery, attraction, mutual trust, and effortless communication."

Signs of chemistry appear as rapid heartbeat, shortness of breath and sensations of excitement that is often similar to sensations associated with danger. Other symptoms include a rise in blood pressure and heart rate, flushing of the skin, face and ears and a feeling of weakness in the knees. One can also feel a sense of obsession over the other person, longing for the day they return or uncontrollably smiling whenever thinking about them.

Don't Get Sucked In And Hypnotized

What's important to understand is what creates all these uncontrollable emotions, so you don't get sucked in and hypnotized into a relationship that you'll regret later on. Or worse, act like a needy little boy and let her walk all over you.

Essentially, if you have chemistry with someone, during year 1-3 of your relationship (depending on the people and circumstances) a virtual explosion of adrenaline-like neurochemicals are created. For instance, PEA or phenylethylamine is a chemical that speeds up the flow of information between nerve cells and flows in abundance during this time.

Also involved in chemistry are dopamine and norepinephrine, which are the chemical cousins of amphetamines... **Yes, Speed**! According to Dr. Helen Fisher, "dopamine produces feelings of euphoria, energy, sleeplessness, and focused attention on your beloved. Biologically speaking, you're experiencing something similar to:

"A Cocaine High"

These three chemicals together combine to give us infatuation or "chemistry." This is the stuff responsible for new lovers euphoria, which allows us to stay up all night talking, have sex 3 times a day and feel like we are walking on air.

Basically, it's a drug we can easily get addicted to and why there are love junkies who jump from relationship to relationship once the chemicals wear off.

Do You Have To Have Chemistry?

Chemistry is important as it creates that initial spark and only happens when two people share the same feelings as mentioned in our description. If you don't have these feelings, there won't be any spark or gush of feel good chemicals to sustain the attraction past the dating phase or even into the dating phase.

Can You Create Chemistry?

If you look at the description of chemistry and ask yourself: Can I create mystery, similarity, attraction, trust and effortless communication, then, of course, the answer is "YES". We'll talk a lot about this later on in Chapter 4 so just keep reading.

Chapter 3 – Clarity Is Power

"Unless we have some deeper common bonds, that magnetic chemistry that brought us together eventually wears off and I lose interest quick." -Erin

Ok so chemistry is absolutely important and we can build our chemistry to a certain degree, but guess what? If you don't get clear about your values before you get addicted to the chemicals of infatuation, you could end up just chasing an illusion of happiness. This illusion usually manifests in one or more of the following three ways:

1) *If I have sex with as many women as possible I will someday fill the void of unhappiness just like all the PUA gurus out there.*

   In reality, the problem here is that don't see behind the scenes when these PUA guys go home and suffer from depression, insomnia and other illnesses. Just like all other addicts, PUA guys don't have control over their weaknesses. They are sex junkies, eternally looking for that next fix that will fix everything but… it never comes.

2) *I just need to be in a relationship, so I don't have to be alone and I can be accepted. So as long as we like each other it will work out.*

The problem here is that many people pick the wrong partner out of desperation. Without genuine connection, the relationship eventually sours. In case you don't already know, national divorce statistics are pushing upwards of 50%.

Most people end up divorced because they never got clear about themselves and what they wanted from a partner. Remember the "love, non-judgment and mutual trust" from our chemistry definition? If you give these away without ever really knowing this person, chances are you'll just stay in the relationship until you receive unbearable pain, at which time you'll either bail out or endure the pain but resent her more and more as time goes on.

Many a man has fallen prey to the trap of being with the wrong woman. Hypnotized by the "Need" for love and sex we find ourselves powerless to the emotions created by our chemistry. We jump into any relationship we can, which a majority of the time ends up being a prison cell relationship where we are virtually tied to a ball and chain. Believe me, I say "we" because I've been chained up several times.

3) *If I'm in a relationship I'll feel pain, they will eventually leave me or they will take up my*

time or they will make me change so why even try.

Sadly, the worse situation of all is that you simply end up alone because you have false beliefs, which most likely came from previous relationships that created a lot of pain. Regardless, we all need love and connection and without them, we will go insane. Just Google it, isolation for extended periods of time will literally drive you insane (Remember Tom Hanks in the movie "Cast Away"?).

The Three Brains

To understand the importance of getting clear before those chemicals of infatuation take over it's important we talk about the evolution of the human brain.

There are three parts to your brain, which have evolved over time, the first of which is the Reptilian or Cave Man brain, widely believed to have developed roughly 50,000 years ago. This is the oldest part of our existing brain and controls life functions such as the autonomic brain, breathing, heart rate, and the fight or flight mechanism.

Lacking language, its impulses are instinctual and ritualistic, concerned with fundamental needs such as survival, physical maintenance, hoarding, dominance and mating. It is also found in lower life forms such as lizards, crocodiles and birds and as such could be marked as the most outdated part of our brain.

As a result of the lizard brain's lower level desires and instinctual behaviors, it causes people to act irrationally and unconsciously make poor decisions. For instance:

- Greed and the prospect of gaining power can lead to purchasing get rich quick schemes.

- Territorial and the prospect of losing space leads can lead to road rage.

- The need for sex and reproduction could lead to epidemic rates of fatherless homes and children being born out of wedlock (currently 43% of US children live without their father).

The reptilian brain is also subject to the law of diminishing returns, so essentially, over time, our brains become accustomed to a stimulus like pornography or Literotica (Think "Five Shades of Grey").

As we are overexposed to a particular stimulus we become desensitized and are forced to seek stronger and stronger stimulation in order to receive a similar pleasurable response.

This is very similar to crack or cocaine addicts who need more and more substance to get the same high, leading to a never-ending vicious and destructive cycle.

Reptilian Attraction Automation

Even though the reptilian brain can send us down the wrong path making potentially poor decisions and ruining our lives, it's also a powerful weapon in your arsenal of attraction. Here's why:

Since the reptilian brain is subconscious (on autopilot) with a primary role of making sure you stay alive and spread your genes, it automatically carries out a set of behavioral responses when presented with external triggers. If we know those triggers we're in like Flynn. And... it doesn't require words; so you can trigger attraction by simply using the right body language and changing your internal chemistry.

Sound too good to be true?

"I don't think a guy has to be really good looking to get noticed, there's a certain way a guy stands and walks that gets a girl to notice." - Eva

"For me to be interested I need to feel a physical presence that communicates I'm strong and confident, its rarely the words he uses that makes me attracted." - Teresa

Let's look at an example. The character James Bond exudes confidence and testosterone (trigger) and the ladies respond with sex (behavior response).

This is powerful stuff when used correctly and we'll talk in detail about the benefits of the reptilian brain and how we can use it to trigger sex and attraction later. For now, it's important to understand that when you fall in love, more often than not, you will overlook the flaws of your partner by viewing them in a predominantly emotional way controlled by your reptilian brain.

But here's the rub. There is no higher level thinking in the reptilian brain that requires compatibility for a sustainable relationship. If it had a voice it might say something like:

"Hey if you're a party animal and I'm a recovering alcoholic trying to stay away from partying, we'll get along great."

Since this infatuation or "In Love" period typically only lasts between 1- 3 years, when it ends, your rational, higher level thinking of the neocortex kicks in. If you haven't gotten clear on your values, beliefs and goals by this time, chances are you'll end up miserable, alone or rejected, pretty much guaranteed!

This is the problem with following most of the dating gurus and pick up artists and using their "systems" to get to a woman or a girlfriend. They don't talk about getting clear and aligned on your values, beliefs and goals before you fall into the hypnosis of attraction.

So how do you think these guys' relationships play out down the road? Think it's possible to rely on sex and manipulation to get past the three-year challenge? Can their system help you reach your 50th anniversary?

Of course not! This is why most of the pickup artists are still single, depressed and deeply unsatisfied, constantly on the prowl for their next fix.

The New Brain

To avoid the trap of falling in love and having it end in misery, rejection or breakup, it's absolutely crucial we use our neocortex to get clear on our higher level, more important values, beliefs and goals. This part of your brain will not only help you 'survive' and reproduce like the Reptilian Brain but it will help you 'thrive' by giving you the power to tap into unlimited abilities and manifest an abundance of health, wealth, happiness and loving relationships in your life.

   This is the evolved conscious section of our brain, which is most in line with source, with our higher self, our true unlimited potential. It generates creation, manifestation, imagination, awareness, development, logical thinking, objectivity, empathy and most importantly - consciousness.

   The Neocortex holds the intellectual capacity for complex rational thought, which has made us theoretically smarter than the rest of the animal kingdom and is the key to becoming a higher evolved, more fulfilled and happier person.

   For example, let's say you've had your eye on a girl, but instead of going for the swan dive between her legs in the first week and blowing your chances of a long term relationship, you put your reptilian brain in check and use the neocortex to hold off and make her want it even more by building tension. Now she wants you so bad she jumps your bones and begs you for sex. We'll talk more about tension and how you can use it shortly, for now, it's important to understand how getting clear ahead of time can save you from years of pain.

Using All Three Brains

Ok hopefully by now you've started to understand the importance of getting clear and how the brain works to your advantage or disadvantage. Whether you're in your 20's and just want to have fun or in your 30's, 40's or beyond and want to get married, this first step in finding your match is listed as number one because it's the most important.

If you don't get this right, it doesn't matter who you meet, how attracted you are to them or how attracted they are to you, eventually, there will be pain and most likely, an eventual breakup.

In this first step, we will set you up for success by getting clear about what it is that you really want, what you're willing to do to get it and how to apply this to your overall marketing plan.

Remember, according to top success and coaching experts like Anthony Robbins, T Harv Eker and Christopher Howard:

"The reason why people don't get what they want is because they don't know what they want."

The RAS

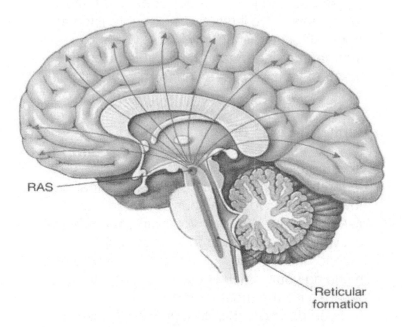

RAS

Reticular
formation

The importance of getting clear cannot be understated and functions hand in hand with our internal homing device called the "reticular activating system" or RAS, which is an actual set of nuclei connected in your brain. The RAS works in conjunction with the law of attraction where you attract what you think about but it's not a secret, it's a real portion of your brain that's been studied extensively.

For example, have you ever bought something like a car or a jacket and thought it was super original, and then you started seeing it everywhere? This is the RAS in action. It automatically seeks out whatever you focus on and brings it to your attention. It's not that the car or jacket wasn't in front of you before; it's that now you've turned on your RAS and are actively looking for it.

But your RAS doesn't just work to bring jackets and cars to your attention. It also works to bring your dream girl to your attention and in some cases your worst nightmare.

For example, let's say Jeremy is really attracted to a blond haired girl who is around 5'4" and looks fit. As such, he finds his RAS constantly looking for these girls and attracting the same type over and over but in the end, it never works out.

This is a common scenario. Jeremy is clear he wants a fit, blond haired girl about 5'4". So why do these girls never work out?

In reality, Jeremy always had at least one major value conflict in each of his prior relationships with blond girls who were around 5'4". Here's the shortlist of conflicts:

- He loved to be outdoors and surf but she loved to be indoors and read books
- He loved beef, lamb and chicken but she was a vegetarian
- He never drank alcohol and she loved to get wasted three nights a week
- He was a strict Hasidic Jew and she was an Atheist.
- He was a giver and she was a taker.

Can you see where this is going? Values and Beliefs override attraction and if you can't align them you're screwed.

So before you go out and get attracted to someone, you'll need to "get clear" on your most important values and beliefs. This is your mental condom, which keeps you from getting hypnotized by your most basic need for sex and love and ending up in the wrong relationship. By getting clear, your RAS will kick into high gear and start locating that ideal match both online and offline. So remember:

Attraction is a poor indicator of long-term sustainability in a relationship.

"My longest relationship was with a guy who I initially didn't have much chemistry with, but we had so many things in common, eventually we fell in love and got married after 3 years."
- Amber

"Every time I go for the guy who makes me weak in the knees, it never works out. It's hot and heavy for a month or two and then it's over because we just never had much in common."
- Jessa

The Clarity Model

Below you'll find the five most important areas of clarity, together they make up "The Clarity Model." As you go through them, get out a piece of paper or launch your word program and write down your own checklist for your ideal match.

Take Action

Make sure you take action here. By writing down your answers, you will make a commitment to make it happen; it will no longer remain just a dream in your head, so don't skip this!

1) **What kind of girl do you want**?

What are her values and beliefs that match yours? These are your "deal makers" or your match from heaven. Write down your top 10 values and beliefs that she must have. For example, she is honest, open minded, always kind and giving, she loves to work out and so do I, she loves to go to church and so do I, she wants to have at least 2 kids and so do I, etc. Now take that list of 10 and shave it down to the top 5 that you absolutely must have.

2) **What kind of woman will never work for you?**

This is your match from hell or your "deal breakers." Write down the top 10 things that would kill the relationship for you. For example, she doesn't like the outdoors and you love it, she is strict Catholic and you just don't believe in Catholicism, she loves alcohol and you don't, she lies, etc. Think about what ruined it in the past for you then pick your top 5 deal breakers and write them down.

3) **Why do you want a girlfriend?**

Reasons push us to never give up and get us there quicker. Write down your top 5 reasons why you want a woman. For example: To have fun, go to movies with, live with someone in a long-term relationship, start a family and have kids, be supported, have sex three times a day (or week), etc.

4) **What do you need to change to attract the girl of your dreams?**

Be honest here or you'll just keep getting the same results. For example, I need to lose about 25 pounds so I'm going to buy the <u>Get Fired Up</u> program today and start working out 3 days a week for the rest of my life. Or, I need to make decent money to support a family one day so I'm going to get a second job or start my own part time business this Monday. Make sure you revisit this question after reading the next chapter.

5) **Make a deadline.**

By what date do you want to be with her? Get clear as if it's already happened and write down your future statement. For example, it's September 21st and I'm sitting down to eat dinner with my new girlfriend. Give yourself 3 – 6 months. This is called future pacing and will kick your RAS in high gear to make it happen much quicker.

In order to turn on your RAS and find her fast, you'll need to focus and take action on these 5 elements daily. So go ahead and write down your answers to the 5 questions above either in your smart phone or on a 3x5 card in a frame. The smartphone is only useful if you can remember to look at these every day otherwise I suggest you put them in a 3x5 frame in your bathroom or nightstand so you can look at them when you wake up and when you go to bed.

Again, this will activate your internal homing device or RAS daily. Trust me on this one, just try it for 3 months and see what happens. I guarantee you will be surprised who shows up in your life.

Chapter 4 – Becoming Irresistible (Your Arsenal Of Attraction)

D o you know what girls are attracted to? Contrary to popular belief, it's not just looks or money and studies clearly indicate that women are attracted to a variety of specific qualities and characteristics.

After polling and interviewing over 2,000 girls and reading several other published studies, I've come up with a top 10 list. As you read this list, be honest and start thinking about where you may fall short and how you can improve.

Top 10 Things Women Are Attracted To:

1) **Fame** – You're in the Public eye (actor, musician, teacher, politician, leader, etc.)

2) **Power** – You are a leader, you have influence over others, etc.

3) **Security** – You possess financial security; give gifts and other material things.

4) **Sex Appeal** – You Look Attractive: Face, Physique, Height, Voice, Hair, Clothes, Posture, Breath, Smell, Body Language, etc.

5) **Self Confidence** – Can do it attitude, take the lead, you don't second guess, ambitious, etc.

6) **Desirable Personality** – You're interesting, humorous, cultured, etc.

7) **Intelligence** – You read a lot, you're well studied and have answers others don't.

8) **Chivalrous** – You open doors, you show respect for peoples' opinions.

9) **Charm / Romance** – You take the time to warm her up with candles, incense, music; you say things that make her feel good about herself.

10) **You Like Kids** – Most women are attracted to men whom they perceive like children.

While some of these like fame and power may be out of your control, these only make a woman feel a certain way, which can be duplicated through the other means of attraction.

You never get a second chance to make a first impression.

While sad, this statement represents the majority of the population. If you don't make a good impression right out of the gate, you could be tossed aside into the rejection pool.

To give yourself the best shot at not only the first but all other impressions, let's go over the top 10 attraction factors one by one to make sure you have the best shot with any woman you encounter.

Fame, Power And Security (Money)

"A guy with no job is like a leaf in the wind, they just float around and I can't take them seriously." - Drisana

It's no big secret that women are attracted to rich, powerful and famous men. A rich man can make a woman feel cherished with material things while a famous man can make a woman feel cherished vicariously through his fame, influence and power.

According to John Grey (Men Are From Mars Women Are From Venus), a woman would willingly trust a famous man enough to have sex with him shortly after meeting because he is already "familiar" to her and trust has already been established.

No wonder why guys want to be famous to the point where they'd sell their soul to the devil.

I intentionally lumped Fame, Power and Money into one group, as they typically are believed to be the ultimate pussy magnets, yet only a small percentage of guys will actually use these to attract a woman.

First, let's get clear on a woman's need for "security." This is the most basic human need for food, shelter, clothing and if you plan on raising a family you'll need to multiply the dollars needed to provide ample security for kids.

So, yes money does matter to a certain degree, but it depends on each person and their beliefs, goals and values as mentioned earlier.

So if you are in high school or college and nobody is expected to have a lot of dough, more often than not, money will not be a big deal breaker.

In contrast, if you have strikingly different upbringings like one of you came from Beverly Hills and uses eats off a silver spoon and the other came from the Brooklyn hood, it could be a deal breaker.

But if you're in the workforce and cool with making $40k a year (and you've done the clarity model), you'll attract a woman who is cool with this as well.

So yes, you need to get clear on your values but it's also important to understand that most women want to know that you can provide some type of security with stable income, especially if you want to raise a family.

If you don't have a stable job or business, this could be a deal breaker, as most women will judge you as if you don't have what it takes to be stable and "secure."

Pain Saver Tip

Note To Pickup Artists - You may have learned some strategies which even I will teach that can activate a woman's reptilian brain and get her to behave in a way that makes her attracted to you even if you are broke and don't consider yourself attractive, but here's the rub:

PUA manipulation techniques eventually, wear off!

So if you or she wants a long-term relationship and you don't have any financial security, you will soon be single again, I can pretty much guarantee it.

For example, when I was in my 20's I stole away a Sports Illustrated magazine cover model from a Rich New York financier by triggering some unconscious behaviors in her but once that stuff wore off, she was back in the New York penthouse drinking champagne with her crusty old comrade.

The Illusion Of Fame Power & Money

This is a good time to dispel the illusion of fame, power and money by being very clear as to their true nature. Once we do this we'll investigate whether or not they can serve the non-famous, non-wealthy people in getting the same trust from girls.

Fame, power and money are not happiness in and of themselves; they only create the illusion of happiness, which is instilled from birth through our conditioning by the media and a very greed driven culture.

To prove this, all you need to do is open a magazine or turn on the television to see some famous, powerful or rich dude put on a pedestal with a $5,000 Armani suit and 3 hot models draped over his arms as if he was to be worshiped like a god; regardless of whether or not he just got a divorce and lost half his fortune to a gold digger. Does the name Donald Trump ring a bell?

As mentioned earlier, the streets of Hollywood are littered with broken hearts and lost souls searching to fill a big hole by jumping from relationship to relationship. The media portrays these people as happy, attractive, intelligent and successful but in reality, it's an illusion as these people are rarely content or satisfied.

This is primarily because their happiness is totally dependent on their popularity - what they look like and how much money they have in the bank. The problem is, these things are constantly changing, so when the money runs out or old age creeps in or they've fallen out of fame, the happiness is gone with it.

Hopefully, this helps put things in perspective so you don't feel like you're missing out. That being said, fame, power and wealth do automatically trigger attraction in women because they make them feel a certain way. So how can we use this to our advantage without falling into the trap of fame, power and money?

Boost Your Passive Value

"Initially I was attracted because people knew him and it intrigued me" – Lauren

Fame is considered "passive value" because it gives you value before you even meet someone. But you don't have to be a movie star or super athlete to build passive value. You can put yourself in the spotlight and build passive value by simply doing things that hold you in the best light among your community. Here are some examples:

- Teach something she likes to learn.
- Practice a hobby that she's interested in and get recognition from the community.
- If you have a video of you doing something cool, like juggling or one of the interesting things you do, post it on Facebook.
- Have your friends talk about your achievements, hobbies and character to someone you're interested in.
- Hold a dinner party and consider doing it often.
- Start or get deeply involved in a charity.
- Organize the annual motorbike rally.
- Start a meetup.com group.

Additionally, you can make a woman feel famous, rich and powerful with other attraction strategies like your confidence, ambition, personality and sex appeal. Let's dive in and see how this works.

The 4 Components of Sex Appeal

Most people confuse sex appeal with just being genetically gifted with a beautiful face and body but even the tall and handsome guy who was born to supermodel parents can't get by on just physical attraction. This is because physical attraction, also known as "static attraction," represents only one of four components to "sex appeal".

So if you aren't over 6 feet tall with a chiseled jawline and perfect body, don't sweat it. With a little effort, you can create irresistible sex appeal. Let's uncover some of these strategies one by one.

Static Attraction

Static attraction concerns the physical features that you're born with and grow into, like your face, height and body type. This is typically THE FIRST thing girls look at, which makes them investigate further or run for the hills.

If you feel this puts you at a disadvantage, don't worry my friend, there's GOOD NEWS! It turns out these things aren't so static after all.

If for instance, you workout and develop a toned physique with larger more defined muscles, your body will change and become stronger. And guess what happens when you become stronger?

Women are helplessly attracted to strong men because it's been genetically programmed into them since caveman days. Remember the primal reptilian brain that needs to be protected and reproduce? As a strong man, you will trigger her unconscious reptilian brain and communicate that you can provide for her and protect her from danger.

On the other hand, if you don't exercise and you eat an excessive amount of carbohydrates, your static appearance will start to change as your belly begins to bulge, perhaps into the shape of a bowling ball, at which point you could even be mistaken for a pregnant woman. You may even develop bags under your eyes (which will most likely be bloodshot) and your skin will look like old leather - 10 years older than it should. Not so attractive, right!

Exercising Is A Game Changer

Exercise may seem unimportant but in reality, it's a game changer, which can totally alter your confidence level, boost your attractiveness and perhaps even save your life if not extend it and make it more enjoyable.
     All girls love guys who are fit! Think about it. Have you ever heard a woman say: "I love my flabby weak man"? Of course not, girls look at your arms, your triceps, your belly and make judgments like:

"If this guy is so weak physically how's he going to take care of me, let alone a family?"

On the flip side, they may think:

"Hmm, he is strong, something draws me to him, I'm interested, at least for sex."

I know it sounds superficial, especially if you've never worked out before, but if you aren't attracting women or the right girl, its time to really step it up and exercise could be one of the simplest ways to really stand out.

To get leverage over yourself and really take action on this it's important you learn the "why" behind the "what." This knowledge and understanding of the massive benefits of exercise will motivate and embolden you to take on a new lifetime habit or simply refine an existing one you may already have.

As you read about the awesomeness of exercise below take note of where you fall short and how you can improve.

"If a guy has a gut, I know it's only going to get worse as he ages. It's really unattractive…" – Angie

"A big reason I keep going back for more sex with my man is that rock hard body I can cling on to when it starts getting rough. It just really turns me on and I'm not afraid to admit that." - Marissa

"I think us ladies like a chest for the very same reason a guy likes a fit, curvy big-breasted woman, it looks good and feels good pressed up against me" – Jennifer

"I like a guy who can wear a tight cut shirt that shows his arms, it really gets me imagining sex with him…." - Juliana

"The first thing I notice is the arms because usually that's all you can see and if they are flabby, it tells me this guy is weak and how is

he going to help pick up the things I can't, or
kids for that matter". –Sarah

1) Exercising increases your energy levels and stamina so you can work more doing the things you love, like making more money, creating art and… having more sex with your new girlfriend.

2) Exercise burns extra fat that weighs you down and makes you slow and lethargic.

3) Working out builds testosterone and human growth hormone (HGH), which gives you more energy, improves sexual performance and libido, helps you sleep better and repairs aging, degenerative body parts.

Ok, decision time. If you're not already working out regularly and building muscle strength throughout your entire body, you're not only missing out on one of the greatest attraction triggers for women but one of the greatest health and confidence builders for men.

Why not give yourself all the advantages you can?

Remember maximum capacity?

It's time to live up to your potential and maximize your chances of attracting and getting beautiful girls to want to date you.

If you really take care of your physical appearance through diet, exercise and sleep, you will look strong, healthy and alert, which translates into attractive, confident, intelligent and trustworthy.

While these attraction boosters are CRITICAL in luring in your prize catch, unfortunately, a detailed exercise training is out of the scope of this book. So instead, I'll share my secret regimen that attracts girls like magnets and keeps me looking and feeling 10 years younger than I am.

It's called *"Get Fired Up"* and it's part of the "Awaken the Warrior Within" training series that I designed specifically for men. This training program combines the unprecedented synergy of three powerful disciplines, which build superhuman strength, tone muscle definition, bold confidence and will increased physical attraction. This includes:

1) Strength training with or without equipment specific exercises to build your testosterone to maximum levels.

2) High Intensity Interval Training with low impact options anyone can do including my 75 year old father. This burns fat in minutes and boosts both testosterone and HGH or human growth hormone, which we just talked about.

3) Yoga makes you the master of your mind while boosting testosterone and lowering your cortisol (high testosterone and low cortisol have been linked to confident leaders).

This program is creating unprecedented results in my clients and there is nothing like it in the world of exercise. With noticeable results in as little as 1 - 3 months, this could be just the program you need to win the woman of your dreams. For more info check it out on our website at:

www.ChadScottCoaching.com/fired-up

Dynamic Attractiveness / Body language

The second type of sex appeal is "dynamic attractiveness," which has to do with the way you express yourself. This represents body language, movements, voice tone, modulation and pausing, which surprisingly accounts for up to 90% of your communication, (10% being verbal through words).

This also brings us back to the Reptilian brain and represents another opportunity to trigger her unconscious attraction and sexual desire, so pay close attention here.

Reptilian Attraction Automation

Studies prove that body language not only dominates our communication but is better understood by women. Since body language is so important to women, it's important we spend a couple of minutes on this topic and up your game another notch.

First, it's important to remember that pick-up lines, language patterns, verbal tricks and gimmicks are NOT enough to close the deal. They might get you googly eyes and a smile but they are a long way away from closing the deal.

Verbal communication only stimulates the CONSCIOUS part of a woman's mind, the high-level, thinking part of her mind that accepts and blocks input based on logic.

For example, if you get a date and try to convince a girl to sleep with you by saying, "Listen baby - I'm the coolest guy you've ever met," don't expect her to start humping your leg.

Your verbal communication is engaging the conscious, logical part of her mind that filters input. Your command is blocked as she says: "Oh great, what a loser!"

But nonverbal communication or body language is not processed by a woman's conscious mind like language is. Nonverbal communication is processed by a woman's reptilian brain.

So if you go up to her and say, "Listen baby, I'm the coolest guy you've ever met," and your BODY LANGUAGE is CONGRUENT with your words, she WILL feel attracted to you and this time she might respond with a sigh of "damn he is hot," not because of what you said, but because of HOW you said it. So remember:

It's your nonverbal cues, the sexual state that you're projecting, which directly bypasses her conscious, critical mind and directly affects her much older, reptilian brain that only feels sex or flight.

By refining your ability to project sexual states, you'll be able to comfortably feel and act sexual around beautiful girls and in turn have beautiful girls feel sexual attraction for you. When this happens you'll be able to use your nonverbal sexual communication to directly bypass the critical walls of a woman's conscious mind and directly touch the reptilian brain underneath it, which responds to sex.

Ok, it's time to get excited because you're about to learn the nonverbal cues of body language, which will help you project a confident and sexual state – without relying on words. Notice the options offered below and how you may currently fall short or need improvement.

- Your smile
- Your stance
- Keeping your body language free and open
- Projecting and controlling your voice

Remember, women are really looking for a "feeling", so if you were to encounter a woman and you wanted to make her feel amazingly rich, recognized and cherished, how would you express it in your voice, your smile and your stride? Let's take each one and break it down:

Your Smile – Studies show that a genuine smile makes you more trustworthy and encourages people to lower their guard. This doesn't mean you need to grin from ear to ear like a goofball unless you are purposely being humorous. Instead, think in terms of a happy and confident smile, as if you won the lottery and 8 supermodels from Victoria Secret want to hang out with you.

"When a guy is smiling at me, it makes me feel comfortable like I know him already."
- Denise

Your Eyes – Looking down conveys to women: "I don't believe in myself, I'm insecure." So unless you need to look away left or right or up to think about something, never look down. Instead, keep your eyes engaged with hers.

Your Posture - The way you sit, stand, and walk can also tell a lot about you.

"Guys who slouch, look like they just got dumped and nobody wants to date a guy who just got dumped." - Brianna

Studies show that roughly 60 - 90% of communication is non-verbal and expressed through your body language. Accordingly, one of the most obvious indicators of whether or not someone suffers from low self-confidence is how they project themselves to the world through non-verbal cues. These include things like eye contact, gait (how you walk), and posture.

While most confidence tools take weeks, months or even years to implement, by deliberately practicing and improving nonverbal cues like posture you can boost your confidence almost instantaneously.

Confidence Postures

As featured in one of the most popular Ted Talks of all time, a study on body language led by researcher Amy Cuddy at Harvard University classified different body positions as "high power" or "low power" poses. In general, the high power poses are open and relaxed while the low power poses are closed and guarded.

"High Power" body language (top row)
vs.
"Low Power" body language (bottom row)
(Images courtesy of Amy Cuddy, Harvard University)

Above you can see an image from the study contrasting high power poses on the top with low power poses on the bottom.

Remarkably, after measuring the testosterone and cortisol levels of 42 students before and after holding both high and low power poses for two minutes, Cuddy found that high power poses increased testosterone by 20 percent and decreased cortisol levels by 25 percent.

This is highly significant since research from Harvard University, The University of Oregon and The University of Texas have discovered that powerful and effective leaders (men and women) not only share similar mindsets, but also similar hormone levels.

More specifically, researchers discovered that: "Powerful leaders tend to have higher levels of testosterone, which leads to more confidence, and lower levels of cortisol, which leads to better coping skills for high stress situations." [i]

The researchers also found that in addition to the common seated and standing power poses, when someone raised their arms over their head like they just won the Olympics their testosterone again shot up by over 20 percent.

If you're at all doubtful about how important good posture is perhaps the following studies will convince you otherwise.

Turns out, over 55 published studies prove poor posture has negative consequences and open expansive posture leads to multiple benefits. Below are five of my favorites; as you read through them, notice which ones relate to your personal circumstances.

Self-Esteem Study

Published by Health Psychology in 2015 researchers state: "Slouchers reported significantly lower self-esteem, mood, and greater fear."

Confidence Study

A 2012 study by scientists Pablo Binol, Richard Petty, and Benjamin Wagner on how body posture might affect "self-evaluation" showed that people who stood in a power pose (they called it "confident posture," with chest pushed out and erect spine) were much more prone to rate themselves more confidently than people in a "doubtful posture," slumped and self-contained.

Low Energy & Body Pain Study

Published in BioFeedback in 2017 by Dr. Erik Peper, this study found that "Sitting up straight" led to "positive thoughts and memories" while a sad, slumped walk "decreased energy levels." The study also found that poor posture could lead to fatigue, headaches, poor concentration, increased muscle tension and even injury to your vertebrae over time.

Power Study

When scientists tried to poke holes in Harvard University professor Amy Cuddy's study from 2012 she created a follow up study published by Sage Journals Psychological Science in 2017. This study examined over 55 additional studies and clearly demonstrates: "A link between expansive, open postures and feelings of power."

Depression Study

A study published by the Journal of Behavior Therapy and Experimental Psychiatry in 2017 found that: "Adopting an upright posture may increase positive affects, reduce fatigue, and decrease self-focus in people with mild-to-moderate depression"

Time For Action

As the ageless adage goes: Proof is in the pudding! And now it's time to eat some pudding so you can really feel the difference in your confidence levels. To do this let's try on a few high power poses and contrast them with some low power poses as follows:

1) First, stand up, cross your arms and ankles while slouching your shoulders forward (see images if unclear). Now hold this low power pose for a good 1 - 2 minutes. Next, hold your arms over your head like you just won the race of your life. Keep going for at least 1-2 minutes and notice any subtle shifts in your emotional state.

2) Next, sit down and cross your arms and ankles while slouching your shoulders forward for 1-2 minutes. Now try putting your arms behind your head and opening your legs as if you just built a $5,000,000 company from scratch and you're basking in the spoils of your success on a beach in Hawaii. Notice any difference? (See image if unclear)

3) Lastly, try the Superman / Superwoman power pose by standing up tall and putting your hands or fists on your waist as if you were superhumanly blocking a thief from kidnapping your baby.   After about 1 - 2 minutes, try the opposite by crossing your arms and rolling your shoulders forward by slouching (see image).   Again, notice the striking difference then go back to the power pose.

Self-Presentation

"I like a guy who pays attention to the little things, like matching his belt to his shoes or his jacket to his hat. It says he's different and unique." - Debbie

The third component of sex appeal is self-presentation, which includes things like grooming, hairstyle, fashion, etc.

If you're interested in attractive girls, keep in mind that they pay attention to the finer details and a few simple modifications may not only make you more attractive but also make up for some of the things that are killing your chances.

So for instance, if you are not six feet tall, but you dress well and take care of your hygiene, you can make up for lack of height (only if tall is one of her criteria).

Circumstances

Research has shown that when we experience the circumstance of heightened arousal, like being on a rollercoaster, we tend to attribute some of the arousal to whomever we are with. Novelty and excitement all drive up the activity of dopamine and norepinephrine in the brain. These neurotransmitters are associated with energy, elation, focused attention and motivation - central traits of romantic love.

So as you do novel things, these chemicals hop into action and may just push you over the threshold to fall in love. Remember though, this can work against you.

For example, if you take her out to some really boring place like Denny's or some dingy bar with really loud music you might not ever see her again.

And if you haven't already thought of it, taking her on a date for a rollercoaster ride is a great idea (if she's into rollercoasters).

So remember, once you get that date (we'll talk about how to close shortly), you'll need to think of a circumstance that is exciting and creates arousal like:

- Rollercoasters

- Live Concerts
- Coffee Bar w/ Couches and cool music
- Comedy Club
- Boat Rides
- Hiking
- Biking
- Play Frisbee
- Take her on the swing set at a local park
- A Scary movie, (once you get to know her a bit) she'll look for you for protection and comfort.

Self Confidence

"What is the #1 thing I'm attracted to in a guy? Definitely confidence!" – Jennifer

"If a guy isn't confident it doesn't matter what he looks like, I'm just not attracted, and have no desire to have sex with him." - Claudia

Ever wish you could just learn how to spark attraction in women without pickup lines, techniques or strategies?

According to my polls, confidence is "The #1 Thing" you have to have in order to keep her interested and want to be with you more.

Ultimate Confidence shows up as a positive energy source that surrounds you and magnetically attracts high quality women automatically. It also makes you stand out from a majority of other men. And this unbreakable confidence will not only work for landing the woman you've had your eye on or the woman you've been looking for, but for everything else in life.

I've personally polled over 2,000 girls on Facebook and over 82% responded with their top attraction factor as confidence. Take a look at the Facebook ad below, then the survey results below that.

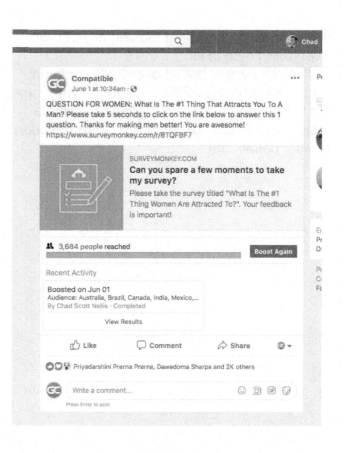

Compatible
June 1 at 10:34am · 🌐

QUESTION FOR WOMEN: What Is The #1 Thing That Attracts You To A Man? Please take 5 seconds to click on the link below to answer this 1 question. Thanks for making men better! You are awesome!
https://www.surveymonkey.com/r/8TQFBF7

SURVEYMONKEY.COM
Can you spare a few moments to take my survey?
Please take the survey titled "What Is The #1 Thing Women Are Attracted To?". Your feedback is important!

🧑 3,684 people reached

Boost Again

Recent Activity

Boosted on Jun 01
Audience: Australia, Brazil, Canada, India, Mexico,...
By Chad Scott Nellis · Completed

View Results

👍 Like   💬 Comment   ↪ Share   😊 ▾

😀😍😮 Priyadarshini Prerna Prerna, Dawadoma Sharpa and 2K others

GC Write a comment...   😊 📷 GIF 🎁

Press Enter to post.

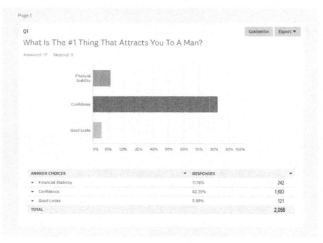

Page 1

Q1

Customize Export ▾

What Is The #1 Thing That Attracts You To A Man?

Answered: 17   Skipped: 0

ANSWER CHOICES	RESPONSES	
Financial Stability	11.76%	242
Confidence	82.35%	1,693
Good Looks	5.88%	121
TOTAL		2,056

55

As you can see, 2,056 women responded to the poll by choosing one of three choices. The results were as follows:

1) Financial Stability   242   - 11.76%
2) **Confidence**   **1693   - 82.35%**
3) Good Looks   121   -5.88%

Clearly, confidence is by far the #1 attraction factor for most women. And if you're worried about not being good looking enough, this should also put a big dent in that false belief.

Even in the media when Hollywood bombshells like Kate Upton, Jordan Rich, Mila Kunis, Eva Mendes, Rihanna and others were asked what they were attracted to most in a man, responded with high-testosterone traits like brute strength, confidence and good health made their hearts flutter. Men without these traits, they said, were weeded out.

If you're thinking maybe you should take a second look at getting physically stronger from a program like *"Get Fired Up,"* you're definitely on the right track.

According to testimonial from Athens Georgia Model Jordan Rich, when asked, "how should a guy approach, she replied:

"He should make his way over to me and have a normal conversation with me. I like confidence. I don't like pick-up lines and I don't need him to think that he has to buy me a drink. That's one of my biggest pet peeves."

Need more proof? 2013's FHM Sexiest Woman Alive, Mila Kunis was quoted as saying:

"Men displaying assertiveness, & confidence" *were likely to win her heart.*

Sports Illustrated swimsuit model, Kate Upton, says she's attracted to:

"Nice guys who are confident and attractive. Confidence is very important, who are you are and what you stand for… that's really attractive to me. If you're yourself and come up and are confident enough to talk to me it's fine. If you're not confident enough to come talk, obviously nothing's gonna come of it because we're not even going to meet."

Why Women Are so Attracted to Men with Confidence.

Remember, according to the subconscious needs of the Reptilian Brain, girls have an unconscious story playing in their heads. They may say they want confident men, but what they really mean is that they subconsciously have the urge to mate with a dominant alpha male.

This again goes back to the reptilian brain, which evolved over thousands of years to encourage women to instinctually mate with the strongest man, (the dominant alpha male). By doing this she would give her offspring the best chance at survival.

Obviously, women want a hero; they want the alpha male, which probably isn't a big secret. It's why superhero movies and comics like Superman, Flash Gordon and Black Panther are so incredibly popular across the world.

The real secret is how can we make you a superhero and attract your greatest prize? Let's talk about the traits of an alpha male. Notice when you read the list where you may fall short or need improvement.

The Alpha Traits:

- A strong sense of self-belief
- Strong physical presence
- The ability and willingness to read people and make decisions
- Cool, calm, and collected demeanor in high-pressure situations
- Social intelligence (the ability to connect and communicate with others)
- Unbreakable Confidence or a strong sense of self-esteem

If there is one overriding lesson that's been handed down from generations of the most enlightened of Sages like Shakyamuni Buddha and Socrates to personal development Masters like Anthony Robbins and T Harv Eker it's this:

"You Are What You Think"

You may have heard this before, but have you ever really taken a moment to really ponder its massive implications?

If you don't think you're confident or in control or attractive or smart or funny, guess what? You won't be!

To be the alpha you must think without hesitation like an alpha.

Now listen closely, because I'm going to tell you something most coaches and gurus simply won't.

While reading this book through to the end is the first step in your understanding and development, it's not going to make you an undefeatable, massively confident alpha male.

Listen, at the end of the day I'd rather have a great testimonial from a guy whose life I changed than another $100 in my bank account. I really mean this, because I also know that anytime I've changed someone's life for the better, they typically are more than happy to invest in more of my teachings anyway. I truly believe "What comes around goes around."

So after you learn the attraction strategies, which are absolutely invaluable, if you feel you'd like to step your game up I've created an entire book and audio series you can listen to at home or in your car called **"Get High On Confidence,"** which is available at: www.ChadScottCoaching.com

Since you are what you think, if you want to attract and land the girl of your dreams, you'll need to think like an alpha, which will require rewiring your brain into the alpha mode, so what comes out of you naturally is pure confidence. I'm talking about a level of confidence you may have never experienced before. Notice if any of the following feels familiar or relates to something you'd like to feel more often.

- Guys respect you unless they are assholes in which case they'll fear you.

- Women stare at you, simply because you radiate confidence.

- You don't need pick up lines because your body language radiates confidence and power.

- You can walk into a room and have the attention of everyone in the room without being a supermodel or saying anything.

There are three main areas for developing confidence, which I talk about in detail in my course "The Winner's Mindset," one of which is Empowered Master Mantras.
Basically, "Empowered Master Mantras" are empowering statements you can say about yourself to begin building confidence and rewiring your brain to alpha level. By repeating these over and over, you'll eventually start to believe and think it.
   If you're at all doubtful of the power of suggestion there have been many scientific studies that prove by faking something over

and over you begin to get good at those very things you were faking.

For example, we already mentioned Amy Cuddy, a scientific researcher from Harvard University. It turns out that part of her research was focused on people faking things they had little experience in. She found that the more these people faked something the better they got at it.

Similarly vocalizing Master Mantras may feel uncomfortable and you may not believe that you represent the words you are saying but if you just keep faking it, eventually you will believe the words and you will feel like an alpha male.

Take Action

To fully understand you must experience this for yourself. So right now I'd like to invite you to drop your guard and suspend any disbelief for a few minutes while you simple repeat the following Mantras out loud repetitively.

- I am courageous and confident. I take the lead and embrace challenges!

- I am a force for good, I am connected to an infinite source of wisdom and power, I take action without hesitation!

- I am calm and confident in the presence of strangers. I speak with charisma and engage women effortlessly.

Did you notice anything, perhaps a boost of confidence, an elevation of mood? Now can you imagine doing this for 10 minutes every day for three months how you would start to feel?

My clients buy my Winner's Mindset course just so they can learn how to do Master Mantras and fully manifest the energy and power of the alpha male. If you struggle with self-confidence and the book just isn't pushing you over the top I highly recommend you check out my master program at the following link: www.ChadScottCoaching.com/winners-mindset

Breaking Desperation & Neediness

Self-confidence is the opposite of "desperate" or "needy," which will definitely kill your chances of attracting a high quality woman.

For example, if you're calling her twice a day, emailing or texting three times a day or looking to get married after the first few months, chances are, you will soon be single.

Whenever you do not receive a call, text or email back, a majority of the time it's simply because you're like every other dude out there - too needy.

If you can avoid this pitfall and she doesn't return your communication, trust assured, it's really not about you. More than likely she's in a relationship, you're not her type (don't be offended), or she's not in the market for a boyfriend at all.

Once you understand the possible reasons for her lack of communication, the most important thing you can do is focus on building yourself and your self-confidence.

If you desire magnetic attraction, first and foremost on this list is breaking any potential neediness. If you think you don't have any neediness, here is a reality check.

To some degree, we all suffer from neediness because we're human. It's not something to be ashamed of.

If you haven't already heard of "failure to thrive syndrome" you may want to look it up. Effectively, if a baby doesn't get tactile (love) stimulation it will die. This is a fact of life, which carries on into adulthood to some degree.

We need love and if we don't' get it we feel as if we will die. So if you're feeling lonely, have heart, it's a natural emotion as a human being.

That being said, neediness is very different from having a built in need for love. Neediness is more equated to insecurity and requires you take action to build confidence in yourself. This topic of building confidence is out of the scope of this book so again, I recommend checking out "The Winners Mindset" if this neediness thing continues to haunt you.

Chapter 5 – Best Places To Meet Beautiful Girls

"Proximity is power!" – Anthony Robbins

Offline Encounters

I f you want to meet a specific type of woman, you need to be "in the proximity of" (near) the places these gals would normally hang out.

For example, if you're into yoga like me you'll be at the yoga studio or at yoga events. These are loaded with hot healthy girls who are, for the most part, stable and love to exercise.

First, revisit your values you listed in the clarity model and determine where girls who have these same values would go.

Next, use the following ideas to meet girls that apply to you.

Note: Some of these places will be totally foreign and completely opposed to your current values. If this is the case, consider expanding into new areas that might actually be good for your health, wealth or spirituality.

Just know that if your intentions are shady, girls will see right through you and reject you.

For example, if you go to a yoga class and you don't have any interest in really advancing your health, but instead you find yourself looking up for a hairy beaver or you're just looking to get laid, girls will see right through you.

Your interest must be genuine and real. With that in mind here is a short list of great places to meet great women:

- Yoga Class
- Dance Class
- Salon or Spas
- Co-ed adult sports league
- Private Parties
- Meetup.com (join groups that fit your values and interests)
- Facebook.com (join groups that fit your values and interests)

Online Dating Sites

Online dating is hands down the easiest way to meet women and doesn't require wasting a ton of time or money trolling for ladies at the local bars.

Statistics from Reuters, Herald News, PC World and the Washington Post show that 76% of all single people in the US alone have opened an online dating profile and it's now socially accepted as "Normal." Even beyond the United States, most developed countries like Europe, Canada and Australia now closely mimic this percentage.

If you're still not convinced online dating is a gold mine, here's a mind-blowing statistic. Did you know that there are 50% more women dating online than men? I don't know about you, but I prefer these odds to the local bar or club scene, which is normally 50% more dudes than ladies.

If we take a look at Match.com as an example, there are 6 girls for every 4 guys. And since statistics tell us there are roughly 72 million women (USA only) who are online looking for dates from only 37 million guys, can your odds get any better?

While there are free and paid sites with a range of options and features they all share the same approach technique we mentioned in the clarity model..

In other words, you will still use the clarity model but it will be employed through the constraints of online dating. So for example, when you craft an online profile you'll be using your clarity model to describe exactly what you're looking for according to your desires, values and goals.

The same applies when it comes to screening. For example, does she share the same values as you, regardless of how hot she is? This is especially important in the online world where you can literally get lost in all the opportunities.

Don't get sucked in the hypnosis of hot women who only look good in a bathing suit. Yes, you may want to have sex with them but they may not share your values and goals. In fact, they may be crazy and you could be falling for a mirage that will suck you into a dry desert with no water... or women. So remember:

Get clear about what you want before the hypnosis kicks in!

When picking an online site just make sure you pick one big enough, otherwise you'll run out of options fast.

Currently, the largest free sites are POF, Bumble, Match and Hinge with the largest paid sites being Match and eHarmony.

Overcoming Online Dating Hurdles

First off, when you meet someone online there is no body language, which as you now know, represents a majority of your communication. All you have is some pictures and written words, which is kind of like flying blind.

Overcoming this is a major challenge, which requires some knowledge and strategy on how to communicate effectively and gain trust.

If you've been online for any amount of time you'll know first hand, without the right strategies, you'll just get rejected. In fact, did you know that according to a statistic from the critically acclaimed book Freakanomics:

"57% of the men who post online dating ads don't receive even 1 email response"

Question: If there are so many women looking for men online, why do a majority of men fail to get past the first email?

Basically, what's happening here is that men are pursuing the women, so the pressure is on the guys to send the first message. Since most first messages are coming from men, each woman is getting anywhere between 5 -

50 men messaging her every day (depending on how hot she is).

Now if you got that many messages, on top of your normal email, texts, and social media, would you read it all?

To make matters worse, most men, write the same stupid, generic, boring emails, which even further reduce your chances of getting read.

Remember: girls DO NOT have time to read all their messages; they only read the ones that stick out.

Since online dating is a entire book unto itself, I did some undercover work by opening fake female profiles on several of the most popular dating sites. My goal was to witness first hand, what mistakes guys were making.

What I found was appalling! Over 80% of all guys did not take the time to craft an engaging profile and roughly 90% blew it on their communication.

Check out some of the most common subject line blunders below. As you read, notice if you do any of these and how you can improve.

- Hi
- Hello
- How are you
- (nothing at all)
- Are you around
- You're Hot
- Hey There
- You are beautiful

Sadly, I used to be the guy who said, "Hey there" in my subject line and couldn't quite figure out why I wasn't getting much response.

Of course, my messaging was equally horrible since I was guilty of engaging one of the worst self-sabotaging atrocities ever to befall a man - apologizing for yourself.

I'm not talking about being responsible and saying sorry when you show up late to pick up your date or forgetting to call her back. No, I'm talking about making comments like, "go easy on me I'm new to this online stuff" or "sorry I didn't write a full description."

What I didn't realize was that I was literally shooting myself in the back. This apologetic attitude makes you look like you don't believe in yourself and what girl is going to believe in you if you don't believe in you? So remember:

Stop apologizing for yourself, it makes you look weak and it's a huge turn off for girls.

Sadly, this is just the start, because if you mess up the picture, the profile or the follow up communication you're equally screwed.

Of course, I found this out the hard way by getting thrown in the rejection pit over and over and over until I'd had enough.

But instead of abandoning it, I took a deep dive into the study of online dating and learned from both sides what makes women go crazy for men online.

What I realized was that there are some key small changes that create massive results in online dating. These I call "Game Changer Quick Tips" and combined with my polling, interviews and reconnaissance have culminated in "Online Dating for Men – The Quick Notes with Game Changer Quick Tips."

This is the bible of online dating, which has helped thousands of guys go from rejected to accepted online and because you've purchased this book, **I'm going to give it to you for free**.

Yes, you could skip to the end of this book and get the details of my offer, but I recommend not getting side tracked.

Instead, just know that it will be waiting for you once you finishing learning the secrets of attracting, speaking and closing the deal on your dream girl.

So let's keep the forward momentum going!

Chapter 6 – Reading The Signals

When you approach a beautiful woman or even think about it, do you tremble with fear and maybe think: "What if she rejects me? Be honest! If this is at all familiar to you, the number one most important asset, here again, is CONFIDENCE.

Since we already covered confidence, in this chapter we'll focus on how to use your confidence to approach any woman with some specific strategies.

First off, it's important to know what she's thinking about the guys who approach her. Here's a typical mindset of a high quality woman:

"Ok he's looking well dressed and I feel a slight attraction, but can he speak, carry a conversation, does he have a spine, is he confident enough to approach me and not be nervous or is he another needy wimp who will do anything for me and I'll get bored of quickly?" - Julie

"Is this guy just another player douche bag who just wants to get in my pants?" - Amber

As you can see, women are looking to invalidate you, so you'll need to prove your worth if you are to get your foot in the door With this in mind, let's talk about some approach strategies and how you can integrate the top 10 attraction factors to approach any girl, any time at any place.

Is She Interested & Single?

Have you ever met someone and just couldn't get a good read on her?

Question: How do you know when a woman is single or interested in you?

There are several ways a woman will drop clues that she's interested and by reading her body language, you'll gain insight, which will tell you how to proceed. Here are some signs to look for:

The Wedding Ring

This is the first thing to look for and the most obvious but some guys don't even know which finger the wedding ring goes on a woman. So here you go: Left hand 4th finger (pinky is considered the 5th).

Body Language

Ok, maybe she doesn't have a ring but what is happening with her body language? Again, body language is the predominant form of communication so getting better at reading it and conveying it should be a top priority for you.

Potential Dating Interest

Below are several body language gestures you may encounter. Notice as you read them if you've experienced them in the past and how you can use them to get a better read on your next encounter.

- **Eye Contact -** The second most obvious sign she's single will be her eye contact, which will be checking you out with short glimpses.

- **Proximity** - Any time a woman is clearly moving closer to you is an invitation to approach.

- **Open Body Language** - If she opens her shoulders and feet towards you and she makes eye contact with you, you've definitely just been given the green light to approach.

- **Questions & Interest** - She asks you questions and her answers to your questions are thorough.

Potential Sexual Interest

If she's really interested and considering you as a potential sexual mate she may exhibit some of the following signs:

- Her pupils dilate.

- She stares at your mouth.
- If she twirls her hair in your presence she could be nervous or sexually aroused by you.
- She laughs at your jokes even when they are not funny.
- She touches you on your arm as a gesture.
- She allows you to touch her with no resistance.
- She uses your name frequently.
- She asks if you are single.

Make sure you look for these signals; they will give you invaluable clues. And don't worry if you're not getting many now. This next chapter will help you generate more interest in both dating and sexual relations.

Chapter 7 - The Crucial 4 (Four Steps To Close)

When first approaching a woman, more often than not, she'll have her guard up. If you want her to respond favorably there are 4 key crucial steps to disarm her and see if there is potential to move further as follows:

1) **Get Into State** – This is your preparation prior to approaching.

2) **Opening Lines** – These are your opening words or level 1 questions.

3) **Question/Qualify** – These are questions to qualify her and get her invested. This includes level 2 and level 3 questions.

4) **Close** – This is where you close and either follow up later or go somewhere else.

Step 1 - Get Into State

Getting into a state is all about creating a "state of mind," which makes you attractive, confident and relaxed before you ever say a word.

While this subject requires a lifetime of study, we'll highlight the foundations to get you well on your way to becoming a natural, without having to use too many words to be successful.

Worst Case Scenario

This is your first preparation strategy prior to approaching. Pay close attention here; this is one of those hidden secrets most people don't know about, which will help you get over fear quite quickly.

When you're feeling fearful of anything that might happen and this fear prevents you from taking action, instead of freaking out, simply do the following:

1) Stop and take 2-3 really deep breaths in through your nose and out through your mouth. This will activate your PNS (parasympathetic nervous system) and instantly slow down your heart rate, which will help you think more clearly.

2) Now think about the worst-case scenario. What is the worst thing that can happen when you approach her?

Once you realize the worst-case scenario isn't that bad, you're fear will dissipate. So in the case of approaching a woman, let's think about the worst thing that can happen. Here are some things she might say:

- Sorry, I'm in a relationship.
- Sorry I have to leave.
- I'm busy right now; please leave me alone.
- She might just turn her head and ignore you.

- If she can't use one of the other excuses, she might just insult you or put you down by calling you a loser. If someone stoops this low, guaranteed they are really unhappy about themselves so don't take it personally. Instead, realize they just saved you from engaging in a potentially painful future relationship.

Now, since someone calling you names can never really hurt you physically, when you read this list, can you honestly say that any of these would threaten your life?

Could you walk away and be the same old dude you were before?

I'd wager you'd notice how freaking easy that was and have more confidence to do it again!

Once you really picture the worst-case scenario and notice how ridiculously benign or non-threatening they are, your fear will melt away if not completely disappear.

Make sure you use this every time you hesitate to approach a woman.

Ok, now that you've let go of any potential fear and you're ready to approach her, you'll need to gauge her interest level and relationship status.

Let's say you're out at the market, an event or even the gas station (it could be anywhere) and you see a woman you'd like to approach. How can you use your body language to gain her interest?

Body Language - How To Approach

"Emotion Comes From Motion"
– Tony Robbins

Every feeling you have emotionally in your body has a corresponding posture, breath and physiology. Your energy is the first thing she'll pick up on when you first see her so it's important to get your body language right here.

"When I'm at a party and a guy walks in and everybody notices, it's usually because he's really confident and acts like a rock star even if he isn't one. – Monique"

Rock Star Entry

Think about Elvis Presley, for a moment. If you've ever watched a video of his you may have noticed how he used body language to make girls scream and lose control more than anyone else.
    Or how about a guy like Justin Bieber? Love him or hate him, undeniably girls scream for him to take his pants off.

Question: What can you learn from Elvis Presley or Justin Bieber, even if you are NOT rich and famous?

Set The Frame And Win The Game

78

When you enter a party, event, club, bar or even a first date you need to set the frame of a bigger picture.

For example, as a singer songwriter I learned that being up on stage is a frame I could use not just when on stage, but when I walked into any place I wanted to meet a woman.

So essentially, I could take that stage presence into just about any bar, club, restaurant, event or date and make myself a magnet for not only women but people in general.

By doing this I would literally have strangers who have never seen me before come up to me and ask me if I was famous. But outside of my small following of fans around the world, most people have no idea who I am.

Since you may not have any reference to what it means to stand on stage with everyone watching you, you'll need to imagine this.

If you're at all doubtful of the power of your imagination consider the following taking from my book "Get High On Confidence":

"Scientists have now proven that when you visualize and imagine something, similar emotions and chemicals are released which create similar effects - as if what you were imagining was actually happening.

For example, one study by Erin M. Shackell and Lionel G. Standing at Bishop's University revealed how it's possible to make nearly identical gains in strength and fitness without lifting a finger!

The study measured the strength gains in three different groups, one of which maintained their usual routine, a second which underwent two weeks of highly focused strength training for one specific muscle, and a third which listened to audio CDs that guided them to imagine themselves going through the same workout as the second group.

Unsurprisingly, the first group saw no gains in strength. But almost miraculously, the third group, which simply imagined exercising, saw a 24% gain in strength compared to the second group (the exercise group) who saw a 28% gain in strength."

Since it's possible to imagine working out and actually gaining muscle in real life, you can also imagine what it's like to be a rock star and experience a powerful state of mind that influences people and makes you more attractive.

To do this, simply watch a commanding performer like Elvis or Frank Sinatra or some more contemporary guys like Bruno Mars or Sting.

After watching for a few minutes close your eyes and imagine you have absorbed their mindset and are now walking into an establishment to meet a lady who thinks you're a rock star.

Now lift your arms over your head like the crowd is cheering you on. If it doesn't feel natural just fake it until it does.

Fake It Till You Become It!

Remember our "fake it till you make it" strategy from Harvard researcher Amy Cuddy mentioned earlier?
You can use this to get into a powerful state and deliver a rock star performance. And the more you fake it, the more real it will become.

Take Action

Right now it's time to put your ego aside, suspend all disbelief and take a few minutes to practice this right now. If you're short on ideas you can use your favorite:

- Rock star
- Athlete
- Superhero
- World Leader
- Entertainer
- Artist

Once you've picked one, you'll need to really imagine what it feels like to be in that person's body. Make sure you answer the following questions:

How powerful do you feel?
What do you see?
Who do you see?
How do people treat you?
What do your friends and family think of you?

Once you really start feeling those powerful feelings, it's time to try this out on a female.

1) First, get clear on the worst-case scenario.

2) Second, step into rock star state by lifting your hands over your head and associating to the feelings of the rock star of your choice.

Remember, body language is 90% of communication, you should know that you are the prize, you set the frame, and you win the game.

Three keys to Rock Star body language are:

Now let's talk specifically about three things, which makes your body language more attractive.

1) **Positive Eye Contact** –Maintain eye contact even if she says something you don't like or doesn't feel good. For instance, if you ask, "do you like dancing" and she says, "no" then pause, but keep eye contact, which will not only hold her attention but also build attraction. Chances are she'll continue to talk or ask you a question.

Place yourself in her shoes, if someone looks down during your conversation and you look away, it would be easy to get sidetracked, but if someone is looking at you and you look away it will be much more difficult to get sidetracked since you know someone is engaging with you.

There are obviously, times to look away like when using humor, but for the most part, you'll maintain positive eye contact. Hold her gaze softly.

2) **Smile** – Make sure you open your heart when you smile. You are your favorite rock star and you want to give love to the world. To test this look in the mirror when you smile. You should see crow's feet on the outer edges of your eyes and it should feel really good.

3) **Your posture** - Do NOT rush in, it triggers the SNS fight or flight response mechanism, which will scare her off. Also, do NOT walk up like a statue or fold your arms. Instead, take your hands out of your pockets, face her with your face, but point one foot towards her and one foot away. This looks impermanent and less threatening, like either one of you could turn away comfortably and leave.

Stop fidgeting - Do you twiddle your fingers, play with your watch or fidget when talking to women? This comes across as nervous and insecure and can hinder your chances. First, get honest and admit it if you do this. Then second, identify the problem and do something different (as mentioned in body language).

Again, you're a rock star, stand up tall, shoulders back, legs and shoulders open to her. Get close enough that she can hear you and makes her think: "This is a man who has a presence and deserves respect, who is he?"

Step 2 – Opening Lines

Ok hopefully at this point you're in state and it's time to open, not with hopes and dreams, but with strategy and preparation. It's time to get her investing in you with some qualifying questions.

Remember, it's not so much about what you say, but how you say it - it's the feeling you put into it that matters. You need to exude confidence from the inside out and get her talking as soon as possible.

Big Tip – The first minute is the most important part of the interaction. Make sure you get prepared ahead of time.

Question: Do you recall the last time you let her get away?

Maybe you were at the market, riding your bike, walking to work, at the café or some other unexpected situation.

Regardless of how she got away, I'd wager it was in the first 60 seconds.

This happens all too often because women show up when you least expect them to, which is also why you need to practice and get prepared before you blow it.

One of the most respected world leaders, Daisaku Ikeda, who has been bestowed over

300 honorary doctorates from prestigious universities and helped millions of people across the globe, once said something that changed my life and I use it for just about everything I do. Listen closely as this could up your game 5 notches.

"Thorough preparation - the kind which allows one to be ready to respond to any contingency - comes a from strong sense of responsibility. Those who think that things will somehow work out of their own accord have already been defeated."

Take Action

The following are some proven opening lines that work in any situation. As you read them take a note on how you could've used these in the past to avoid previous blunders.

Next, open up your smartphone and write down your favorites for easy access in the future.

Lastly, read your favorites out loud to yourself at least 5 times. This will begin the process of auto-recall so you don't fumble the ball next time she shows up.

If you do forget, you've always got quick access to them on your phone.

The Three Levels Of Conversation

Generally speaking, there are three levels of communication with words (not including body language), which will gain more and more trust.

Level 1 Questions (Location / Occasion)

The first thing you say to a woman will depend on where you are and what she is doing.
These are your Level 1 opening line questions.
For the most part, your best opening line will simply introduce yourself and ask a question about your location or the occasion.
For example:

Hey, how's it going? What brought you here today?

"I can't stand it when guys come up and say cheesy pickup lines. It's like they've been living in their parent's basement and haven't been out of the house in 5 years." Jessica

When pick up lines don't work its usually because they are not genuine, not funny, or just plain cheesy. Most girls see right through disingenuous communication.
That being said, there are certain situations where "Hey how's it going" just won't be as effective during awkward moments, like when she's at the market or on her way to catch a cab.
Or you may want to try humor, which when delivered sincerely, can be extremely effective.

To make the awkward moments smooth and easy I've listed some of the most time-tested lines below.

As you go over these approach methods you'll see some indirect conversation starters and some direct "Hey I'm interested," openers. As a rule of thumb, if she's alone and looking at you or you're getting a good vibe, go for the direct opener. And if you're really unsure, go for the indirect openers (more on this in a minute).

Solo Approach (Direct Opener)

Sometimes being direct is really appreciated by women; it's honest and cuts straight to the truth - I'm interested.

If you use one of these, you'll need to be really confident and unwavering in your delivery. Yes, you could get shot down quick but you also don't want to waste valuable time on someone who just isn't going to work out no matter what you do or say. Let's take a look at some examples:

- "I saw you when I first walked in and thought, If don't at least say hi I'd be kicking myself for a week. I'm (fill in your name), what's your name?

This last one worked for me when I was rollerblading down the boardwalk near the beach one day. I was cruising pretty fast and saw this beautiful girl standing alone looking around so I turned around, skated right up to her and said:

"I saw you as I was flying by and thought... if I don't turn around and at least say hi I'd be kicking myself all day. I'm Chad, what's your name?

She said: "I'm Danielle," with a huge welcoming smile. After about 5 minutes of conversation, I closed and ended up meeting her and her friends later that week. This one works great when you're on the fly.

In a separate encounter, I had just arrived in Nicaragua to write a new book and was walking down the beach. Out of the water came a beautiful local girl in a string bikini. It was almost surreal, she was stunning, like the movie "10" with Bo Derrick.

Fortunately, since I practice this stuff I was prepared and walked straight up to her and asked:

"Habla Ingles?"

Fortunately, she spoke English so I asked:

"I noticed a lot of people come to this establishment, do you know if this is a surf camp?"

Once she answered, I simply continued talking about the location by asking more questions, which then led to asking her questions about herself like:

"Do you surf?"

When she said no, it actually opened the door to:

"What do you love to do?"

Eventually, I closed by asking for her WhatsApp info and she ended up being my girlfriend for two months while I lived in Nicaragua.

Opinion Openers

The opinion opener approach works like a charm and involves picking a topic of interest and either approaching solo or with a wingman and asking for her opinion. This is less intrusive and engages her on a non-threatening level; especially if it's about a subject she can dig her teeth into like music, sex, dieting, hair, spas or other chick stuff.
     To get her opinion, simply create a topic you are curious about or if you have a wingman something you two disagree on. To get the answer you simply ask the question to a group of ladies or an individual standing nearby. Here are a couple of examples:

The Proposal

"You look like someone who could help us with a little dispute. My buddy has been dating this gal for six months and wants to propose. How soon is too soon to get engaged?"

The Ex-Girlfriend

"Hey ladies can I get your opinion on something? My buddy just moved in with his girlfriend and when his ex-girlfriend who he's remained friends with calls she gets all hot and bothered. How do you feel about that... justified or not?"

The Palm Reader

"Hey, my buddy says he knows how to read palms but I think he's full of shit. Since he knows everything about me how about donating your hand for a quick read?

You can escalate much quicker by using an excuse like palm reading or another respectable kind of physical touch.

Naturally, you'll need to know how to do a little bit of palm reading if you're going to use this one, which you can figure out simply by looking online.

It's also important to note that by touching her hand you've escalated quicker towards potential kissing and getting intimate.

If she's skeptical you could use an objection rebuttal for any of these options. Here's an example:

The Rebuttal

"I used to be skeptical too but my uncle pointed out a few lines on my hand and he was dead on in his analysis so he taught me a few things about reading palms. Hey, you got nothing to lose, can I see your hand."

Step 3 - Question/Qualify

This 3rd step of the "Crucial 4 to Close" is all about good questions that help you gain trust and rapport. These include both level 2 and level 3 questions.

Level 2 Questions - Career / Passion

Now once you get the introduction over its time to dive into some conversation. In the initial 5-15 minutes of your conversation, you'll mostly be using level 2 questions that usually relate to her career and passions.

Keep in mind, some people aren't very passionate about their careers so it's best to start with passions.

Also, try not to barrage her with an endless stream of questions. This causes stress, like a police interrogation, when in reality she's probably just looking to have fun.

When in doubt, just remember to expand on each question and connect it to something else of interest. This is called a conversation catalyst.

Conversation Catalysts

During your conversation you want to be thinking: "What question or topic does her last answer bring up." One thing leads to another so let's take a look at a few catalysts that spark more interesting, trust building conversation.

Encourage her to talk about herself

Be a good listener and let her do most of the talking. Remember that a person's name is to that person the sweetest and most important sound in any language. Example: "So Emma, what do you love to do most?" "Tell me Emma, what are you most passionate about?"

For example, if you ask her what she's passionate about and she says helping rescue dogs, then ask:

"What is the best part of rescuing dogs?"

Or

"What about rescuing dogs gives you the most joy?"

Challenge Her

After you've got a sign that she's interested, you can develop more interest by challenging her on one of her opinions or interests. This works especially well for women who always get their way.

If she is hot, chances are most guys agree with everything she says, which is a great opportunity for you to be different and challenge her.

On the other hand, if she is shy and reserved you want to be careful as you might scare her off.

For example, if she says, "I'm passionate about saving pine trees and poison arrow frogs", you could say:

"Since the advent of the computer and electronic storage, pine trees are not in demand like they used to be. What about supporting something that helps people learn why they have such tendencies towards violence and destruction that they would actually chop down trees in the first place?"

Since most guys would just simply go along with her interests even if they had no interest in what she's talking about, she's most likely going to reject all of these guys and be more interested in someone who actually challenges her.

If she doesn't like to be challenged, chances are, she's extremely insecure and probably not someone you want to spend a whole lot of time with.

"When a guy spends most of his time complimenting me and agreeing with me, this is a red flag that signals, I just want to bang you and I have no opinion of my own." - Paula

Obviously, this doesn't play to your favor so be on the lookout for people pleasing.

Later on, after you challenged her on one of her opinions or interests, if you compliment her, that compliment will have way more weight. So remember to be open and honest and never a kiss ass as it makes you look weak.

Instead, remember that you are the selector, NOT the selectee. Take the position of power and make her jump through your hoops. Since this is so important I'm going to repeat it:

Take the position of power and make her jump through your hoops!

Here are a few ways to actively issue a challenge:

- I think all women are beautiful, so what talents do you possess that make you more attractive to others?

- If you could wake up tomorrow any place on the planet where would it be?

- What's the one thing you can't say no to? This will lead her towards desire and desire for more. Hopefully, a desire for you!

- What talents do you have that would surprise me? Question: What surprising talent do you have? Don't move on until you can answer this question.

- Have you ever been in love? This will help her to imagine being in love with you.

Essentially, you want to ask these questions until you get to the point where she says:

"I feel like I've known you forever."

This will only happen if you are very confident, relaxed, open and warm, which will make her feel comfortable around you. So if you struggle with confidence and self-worth make sure you look into the booster recommendations at the end of this book.

Step 4 - The Close

Alas, step number four in "The Crucial 4." This is the crucial moment where most guys blow it and fumble the ball so pay extra close attention here.

End It First

The first thing to remember about closing is to make sure you end it before she does. This has two important psychological implications for women.

First, it says, "I'm not needy, I'm really busy and if you want me, you'll have to work hard."

Second, it says, "I'm in the driver's seat, I'm in control," which women are attracted to (remember the alpha male).

Women love the chase, they want what they can't have and they spend a lot of time wondering if you really love them. To keep her on her toes and end it first.

Depending on the circumstances, some closes will be different from others.

For example, you might be closing for a number, a kiss or a one-nighter, which all require different closes, so let's go ahead and familiar with the possibilities.

Phone Vs. Email

Most guys think that if you have her phone number you are golden, but the reality is that girls will respond to a brand new connection through a text or email more often than through a phone message. So your first option should always be a phone number.

If for some reason she doesn't want to give out her phone number or you don't know if you are super interested but you want to check her out further then ask for a social media profile or email address.

Keep in mind, girls give their phone out to lots of guys because they know its safe, they can always block your number. But even more perplexing is the fact that some women have already decided they won't call you back before you even call.

"If a guy is a player I might give him my number, but I've already decided not to call him back. It's just kind of a game girls play to get attention." - Pricilla

Fortunately, if you have the right text message or email subject, you can get it delivered to just about anyone.

Another big blunder guys make before asking for digits is not building enough trust.

"I really hate it when a guy just asks me for my phone number and I know nothing about him." - Kimberly

In order to avoid this, you'll need to use specific rapport builders with level 2 and 3 questions.

For example, let's say you talked for around five minutes and you've got her interested or made her laugh, and you say:

"It was nice to meet you, I need to go entertain my friends, let's exchange information."

If she says NO, then ask:

"Do you have an email address or social media profile?"

Then when she says yes, you can treat this yes as a "yes I will give it to you" and simply follow up with, "What is it?"

Lead Her (Indirect Close)

A really simple and safe way to get her info is to think about a great restaurant, club, bar, game or park with a fun environment and talk about it with her. Here are some examples:

The Sushi Bar / Fun Restaurant
Sushi and other fun restaurants are always a great option because of the lively atmosphere.

M: Have you heard of the sushi bar Kamikaze?

W: No

M: It's got some of the best and freshest sushi in town and they play really fun house music. I'm going there next weekend with some friends; you should join us.

W: Yeah that sounds fun; I'll have to check my schedule.

M: Great, lets exchange info and I'll text you the details.

The Museum
Pick something you've wanted to do, see or try, like a new restaurant/bar/museum/etc. and ask her:

M: Have you been to Balboa Park Museum? They have the most amazing gardens.

W: No I haven't been in probably 3 years.

M: Neither have I, we should go.

W: Yeah that sounds lovely

M: Great, lets exchange info

Get the idea? Never just ask for the number, instead, make it a natural progression of the relationship building process.

You've met her and talked to her, asked some level 1, 2, and 3 questions and now you've brought up a suggestion that hopefully matches her passions, at which point you simply ask her to join you.

To avoid her flaking on you, make a tentative date for the adventure by actually scheduling it! This way she'll be thinking about it all week until you call and she'll be less inclined to back out.

When It's Inconvenient

If your conversation is short and one or both parties don't have time, there are some very specific strategies you can use.

For example, let's say she's in line at the market or she's at the gym working out. First, you would use location or occasion to open and to close you would follow this example:

M: Great talking, we should continue this conversation sometime.

W: Sounds good

M: Cool, just put your number in here (Hand her your phone ready for numbers).

Daytime Strategies

Unlike nighttime encounters where women are constantly getting hit on, a daytime encounter will give you a much better chance at genuinely connecting with a sober girl who doesn't have her guard up.

Also, daytime opportunities allow you to meet women who never even visit a bar or club and could potentially be much better for long-term relationships.

The first obvious challenge during the day is that women are busy and they typically are not expecting or looking to meet anyone. This is where you'll need to use an excuse to speak while using natural spontaneous openers.

For example, if you see a girl walking toward you, you can make eye contact and put up an imaginary stop sign with your hand when she's about 10-15 feet away to give her time to stop. If she's intrigued, you have about 3 seconds to engage and see if she's interested in what you have to say.

Don't say excuse me, as this sounds like a homeless guy asking for something. Instead say:

"Hey, (pause while she stops) I need to ask you a question."

This question can be related to the store, the gym, her hair or anything genuine that could be of interest to her.

Since most people are primarily concerned with themselves, one of the best questions is a question about her or what might benefit her, like a compliment or a suggestion. This interaction should be around 5-15 minutes, which includes three parts as follows:

1) **Open** – These are your first words where you stop her in her tracks with something simple.

2) **Connect** – This is where you introduce yourself and talk about something that you're both interested in, but this could carry over from the Opener.

3) **Close** – This is a quick close for info exchange with an excuse to leave.

Below are a few examples. Make sure you write these down if they strike you as something you could use on the fly.

Something She's Wearing

Open

M: "Hey (pause) I love your yoga pants, has anyone ever told you they look like the jungle in Costa Rica... have you been? "

W: "Oh thanks, no I've never been."

M: "Its one of the most beautiful places I've ever been, you should definitely go someday." Where do you practice yoga?

W: "Yoga One downtown"

Connect

M: "What's your name?

W: "Anna"

M: "I'm Chad nice to meet you, I love yoga one have you tried Yoga Six in Point Loma?"

W: No

M: "Well there's a great class on Wed and Friday by an amazing teacher, you should come."

W: "Sounds amazing"

Close

M: "Cool, I gotta run why don't we exchange info and I'll text you the details."

Get Directions

This could be you solo or with a friend. Start off with an excuse to talk like getting directions to someplace in the area.

Open

M: Hey, do you girls know where the Pink Lady Is?

W: Yes it's just up the street / No sorry

M: You look like you're headed somewhere fun, do you mind if I ask where you're going?

W: We're headed to the Karaoke bar on 5th St.

M: Oh that sounds way more fun than the Pink Lady, do you mind if we follow your lead?

W: Sure no problem

Connect

M: Great what's your name? (Exchange name and connect on common interests)

M: So are you professional singers… are we going to be witnessing the next American Idol?

Etc.

Close

At this point, you're at the karaoke bar and you've established more rapport by possibly singing or dancing or other banter with these girls. There are several scenarios that can pan out at this point. You could single out one of the girls and start to escalate or you could just get a number and close.

M: Hey thanks for the laughs, we gotta meet a group of friends, but we should do this again.

W: Yeah sure

M: Great lets exchange info. Go ahead and put your number in here (Hand her your phone with her name already programmed).

The Daytime Tourist

If you see someone in the day, it would be difficult but not impossible to escalate to an immediate date. So you'll need to feel it out. If she's clearly on schedule and needs to be somewhere try something like this:

Open

M: Hey do you know where the Pet Co Stadium is?

W: Yes, it's up the street one block North and two blocks South.

M: You give great instructions; I should hire you as my tour guide.

W: Thanks

Connect

M: One more quick question… what's your name?

W: Jennifer

M: I'm Chad, you look pretty hip, what restaurants do you suggest for sushi?

W: Try Riki Sushi

Close

M: That sounds perfect, I'm meeting up with a friend and we'll probably head over later, then go to a party. Would you like to join us at either?

W: Sure/Maybe

M: Ok great lets exchange info and I'll send you the details.

W: I have plans but thanks

M: No worries, you seem pretty cool maybe we can connect another time. Are you on Facebook or Instagram? (Get info)

This close assumes a "no" so it's a softer approach. If on the other hand, she says yes you'll be asking for her phone number to text her later.

Level 3 Questions – Past, Pleasant Childhood Experiences & Spiritual Beliefs

Ok, now that you've established some trust with level 1 and level 2 questions it's time to get excited because I'm about to share some level 3, top-secret language techniques that quickly build deep bonds. This is the stuff that makes her feel like she's known you for her whole life.

Just make sure you do not use these prematurely, as they are typically effective only after you've gotten past introductions and gained a little trust.

Essentially, past childhood experiences that are pleasant represent some of the most powerful experiences we have and Spiritual beliefs are the deepest beliefs we have.

When you start asking questions about old experiences or spiritual beliefs, the further back you go in time, the deeper your bond will become.

Keep in mind, if she has spiritual beliefs that you don't, proceed with caution, as this could be a deal breaker. Let's look at a couple of examples.

Old Childhood Experiences

M: I'm very curious about something, where did you grow up and what games did you play when you were a kid?

W: I had this great bike I rode all the time.

M: Was it a girly bike or a BMX?

Spiritual Connection

M: What do you do on Sundays?

W: I go to a Jewish/Christian/Muslim/Buddhist synagogue

M: No way, I'm Jewish/Christian/Muslim/Buddhist too, what keeps you going back?

Keep talking about the subject and let her recall her memories, while you draw parallels to your life.

Overall 3rd level questions are about digging for gold nuggets that matter most to her. In other words, what really lights her fire and gets her talking endlessly?

Your quest is that of a miner, looking for the gems and precious metals that she's most passionate about. In fact, one of the simplest questions you can ask is:

"What really lights your fire?"

You can use these level 3 questions as part of your closing sequence but again, just make sure you've gained some trust with level 1 and level 2 questions before you lay on the heavy stuff.

Chapter 8 – Follow Up and Get The Date

At this point, you've used "The Crucial 4" and maybe you've even gotten physical depending on the situation. Now is the time to follow up and go on a date.

"I can't stand it when a guy just keeps calling all the time, it's like a needy dog that won't go away." – Jamie

On The Phone

Remember that women (especially beautiful ones) get a lot of attention and if you just act like a needy dog by calling her right away or too frequently, you'll more than likely just get rejected.

Instead of falling into this trap, wait before reaching out. This is completely subjective to the circumstance so you'll have to gauge each situation separately.

For example, if you told her you were getting together with friends that night or going to a party that night, you'd obviously need to communicate with her the same day regarding the details. If this is the case, you still want to resist any temptation to be overly excited and look needy, so instead of waiting days perhaps you simply wait an hour or two.

If on the other hand you met her at the market and just wanted to follow up for a date, you would want to wait long enough to build some tension but not so long that she forgets about you or thinks you really don't care. Typically this will be around 1-3 days at which point you can send her a text message with the goal of either building more trust with a phone call or going straight for the date.

Again, this will be completely subjective to the circumstance. So if you feel there is no way in hell she's going to go on a date without building more trust or you don't feel you got a good read on her, then shoot for a phone conversation.

For example: "Hey Jen, it was great meeting you, let's jump on a call. Let me know if you are available Wednesday or Thursday night."

If on the other hand you got a good read and think she'll respond well to a date then send a text.

For example, "Hey Jen, I really enjoyed your good vibrations and would love to grab some coffee or a drink. Let me know if you're available on Thursday night or Sunday during the day."

Keep in mind these days I've suggested are very strategic. They are low pressure days and don't commit her to the high value nights like Saturday.

Get Into State Before You Call

If you haven't built a lot of trust yet there's a good chance you'll be nervous when you call her. Do NOT call her until you get rid of the nerves. Here's what to do:

Imagine She's A Good Friend - Close your eyes and imagine she is a good female friend whom you haven't spoken to in a while but known since childhood.

Move Your Body - Next shake out the nerves by doing about 10 jumping jacks and 10 pushups. This will immediately disperse any negative or anxious energy and put you in a state with a much higher vibration, which she'll feel as confident and attractive.

Remember, you need to make her jump through your hoops. Unless you're feeling you have a great connection, don't let it drag on more than 15 to 30 minutes. This will give you enough time to determine if you want to actually take her on a date.

If you get any red alarms like she's crazy, selfish or just wants a free meal end it by saying:

"Hey I have a ton of work to do can we talk another time?"

Don't worry about calling her back; you're off the hook my friend. Besides, she's most likely got other dudes calling her.

On the flip side, if you're feeling a maybe or better, go for the date. Here is an example of a closing sequence to set up a date:

- "Hey listen, I'd love to chat more but I have to take off, why don't we continue this conversation in person over some coffee or tea?" (Sound busy, not needy)

- "I know of a great spot over on Turner Street." (Next to some eclectic shopping or rollercoaster to get her excited)

- "How is Thursday night?" (Be specific and don't give her a lot of options, make her jump through your hoops)

What If She Doesn't Answer The Phone?

1) Make sure you leave a voicemail and don't block your number.

2) Speak to her like you have known her for a while by saying something like: "Hi it's Dave."
3) Use some references to the conversation you first shared. For example, if you had a nickname for her, call her by that name. Don't run on for 3 minutes, make it 1 minute or less.
4) Close by using a reason for her to call you back. For example, you have a funny story; you need her female expertise, you wanted to invite her to a really cool party, restaurant, event, hike, etc.

What If She Doesn't Call Back?

If she doesn't call back after one message, she may just be busy. Wait one full week then leave another message.

Keep in mind I take a deeper dive into online messaging and texting in my book "Online Dating For Men" so make sure you get your free copy at the end of this book.

Chapter 9 – Dating & Building Trust

If you've integrated the suggestion so far and taken the requested action, you should start to notice some different results in how women respond to you. Perhaps you've even met someone you're really excited about.

Just keep in mind, there are several variables involved which could blindside you and send you back to the couch alone, so we'll address those with some more trust building and heart winning strategies.

Best Date Locations

"Big turn off for me, is when he does not take the time to plan out a date and think of something different, it's like I'm disposable." – Amber

When it comes to the best date locations, we'll need to revisit "Circumstances" in Sex Appeal, as this will help her get really excited about you.

If you recall, circumstances create feelings, which are then associated with you. For example, if you take her on a rollercoaster and she gets so excited she wets her panties, she may just jump your bones at the end of the night. Don't count on it, but it has happened before.

And while there may be only a few of these circumstances you can use for the first date, like a hike, a cool coffee shop or some exciting activity like a rollercoaster, for the rest of these circumstance locations, you'll want to use them as a follow up date.

For the first date, you can still get good circumstances with a well-chosen café with character. Just make sure it does not have loud music that makes it difficult to hear each other.

To get some great ideas use www.yelp.com or other review sites and make sure the location is going add to the experience rather than take away or make you look boring.

Body Language

"Any time I see a guy with great posture, I'm drawn and attracted for some unexplainable reason, I want to know more about him." - Kelly

When you meet in person you'll be using your smile, stance, posture, voice and dominant actions as discussed in Sex Appeal "Dynamic Attraction." This is game time, so you'll need to step your game up by revisiting that section and working on your body language before you go on a date.

Most importantly, greet her with a hug, not a handshake. This communicates, "I'm warm, lovable and friendly," and will encourage her to drop her guard.

Make sure you stand tall, and when you sit down, sit upright without slouching. Relax and open your legs and posture like you're the most confident rock star on the planet.

As far as dominant actions, I recommend you meet her at the date location but don't be early, instead be either right on time or a minute or two late.

Also, be a gentleman but don't be needy. In other words, open doors for her, give her the best seat and order for her, but never complain or apologize for unnecessary things.

Stay Focused - It may be tempting to look at other girls, especially if a hot one walks by. Don't do this, it says, "I'm a player and I don't care much about you." Instead, resist this temptation and stay focused on your date. Looking at other girls also tells her you're probably not very loyal so why would she ever want to have a long-term relationship with you. If you're not into her we'll talk about how to get out early very shortly.

Mind Your Manners - Girls are really turned off by men who are slobs. Make sure you eat with your mouth closed and don't talk with food in your mouth.

"Men who eat with their mouth open or pick their teeth gross me out and sexually it's a huge turn-off, I have no interest in kissing or sex." – Rebecca

Conversation Questions

"There's nothing worse than that uncomfortable pause and the conversation dries up." – Briana

If you recall from level 1,2,3 questions, one of the most important things to do is get her talking about herself. Since most guys blow it here, I've listed some great level 2 questions with a few level 3 questions sprinkled in at the end to help you prepare ahead of time.

Take Action

As you read these questions, notice which ones appeal most to you and write them down in your smart phone for quick access and regular practice.

Men Vs. Women

- What is the sexiest body part of a man?

- Do women really mean what they say or do they say they want something but really deep down want something else? And what evolutionary purpose does this serve?

- Are women attracted to men who are really masculine? For instance, do you like guys who are physically fit or guys with a lot of hair on their face?

Humor

- What really makes you laugh?

- What is the funniest movie you've ever seen?

- Who is the best comedian in the world, dead or alive?

- Who is the funniest person you know? Why?

Adventure / Food / Music

- What's your favorite place in the entire world?

- What's the most scrumptious dessert on the planet?

- What do you think about the ocean, the mountains or rain?

- What is your most favorite restaurant and why?

- What would be the most ideal vacation for you?

- Been to any cool live music concerts lately?

- What do you have on your iPod these days?

- Would you ever scuba dive? Surf? Snorkel?

About Her – Qualify

Too many qualifying questions can make it sound like an interview or interrogation so sprinkle these in occasionally but make sure you ask some important questions as well, otherwise you may be wasting your time.

- What are you most passionate about?

- How would you describe yourself?

- What do you do to relax or de-stress (find out her level of health)

- If you had $10 million in the bank and never had to worry about money what would you do with your days?

- What does a great weekday look like for you? How about a weekend?

- What are your biggest goals in life right now? What about future goals?

- What do you eat on a daily basis?

- Do you have a nickname? Tell me the backstory

- Do you have any pet peeves?

Level 3 – Bond

- What was your family like growing up?

- What was your favorite thing to do as a kid?

- Do you have a religious or spiritual practice?

Escalate the Conversation

If you recall from earlier we talked about how to build the conversation by digging for gold nuggets. It's game time now so you'll need to keep her talking by asking questions about the stuff she is already talking about.

For example, if you ask her what she loved to do as a kid and she says: "I used to love staring at the stars," you can follow that with:

"What was that like for you?"

Or

"Why did you do that?"

Keep her qualifying herself and make her jump through your hoops!

Escalate The Excitement

If it's your first date and things are going well, don't sit for more than 30 to 60 minutes.

The problem with sitting for long periods is that it lowers your vibration, makes you slow, boring and lethargic - not to mention uncomfortable.

Instead, after you've had a beverage ask her:

"Hey why don't we take a walk and check out the local shops."

This will create excitement and you'll have more to talk about.

If there happens to be a rollercoaster, Ferris wheel or arcade where you can compete against each other (drive a racecar, throw baseballs to win a stuffed animal) go for it, these are big excitement builders.

Consider taking her on a boat ride, a beach walk, rent bikes, get on the local swing set, or anything that is not just sitting and talking.

Remember, this excitement of the circumstances gets attached to you and makes you more exciting and attractive. Don't skip this one!

End It First

Again we covered this earlier, but it's super important to convey you are not needy and make her jump through your hoops.

To do this, make sure you end the date before she does as the moment you end it there will be tension, which will remain until you see her again. This means she'll want to see you even if she has no idea why.

If you're not into her, be polite but don't drag it out and waste time. Here's a quick exit example:

"Hey listen I have another commitment I need to attend to, why don't we catch up another time."

Again, you owe her nothing so don't feel bad about not following up. You need to focus on finding the right girl. Better to move on and not waste your valuable time and money.

If it went well and you know you want to go on another date make sure you end it with a preview of a future date, which will get her even more excited. For example:

"Hey, I really enjoyed our time together, you have really good energy, let's do it again soon. Maybe we can go on that hike to Sherman Peak we talked about."

Again, build tension by waiting a day or two to follow up. Additionally, continue using circumstances and other attraction items from the Top 10 Attraction Factors to build more tension.

Chapter 10 – Loyal & Committed

"Most guys have no clue how to warm up to sex, they just want to dive in. Girls are different, we need a little romance." - Roxanne

You may have heard of Kino Escalation as some secret sex technique used by pick up artists but its really only part of a bigger more important picture – keeping your girl committed.

If you're reading this book I'm going to assume you're more interested in finding a girlfriend than just learning how to have sex with as many women as possible.

The fact is, if your goal is the endless pursuit of sexual partners, you're really just a couple steps away from a crack addict – no matter how high you get, it's never high enough.

But Kino is just scratching the surface when it comes to keeping a girlfriend as this will simply provide you with the tools to escalate into a sexual experience and typically does not address the trust building and relationship bonding aspects of a relationship.

In other words, it's not for manipulation purposes; rather, it's really a tool for helping you build more trust and winning her heart. Make sure you keep this in mind as we explore the intricacies of Kino escalation.

Now depending on what your goals are, there are basically 7 stages to get her from stranger to sex as follows:

1) Positive Eye contact
2) Verbal communication face to face
3) Hands-on embracing caressing or massaging
4) Mouth to mouth contact – Swapping Spit
5) Hand to genital contact (could also be mouth to breast contact)
6) Mouth to genital contact – Oral sex
7) Sex – Dipping the Big Dipper

Amazingly, most men go their whole lives without ever being taught this and most have no idea how they are making things much more difficult than they need to be.

Thankfully, once you understand the seven steps of Kino, dating and sexual communication become a lot easier. Once you can recognize what step you're on and where you need to go, the courtship becomes a dance rather than a frustration fest.

Obviously, steps 1, 2, 3 and 4 are pretty elementary, but if you find you got shut out somewhere, go back and review these. Chances are you skipped a step and she just wasn't ready or got freaked out because you were going straight for the swan dive between her legs.

If you're seeking a long-term girlfriend, by skipping a step you may find yourself in an embarrassing situation or worse – slapped in the face. The keyword to remember here is:

Patience!

Again, you'll want to revisit your goals and determine if you just want to have fun or if you want a serious relationship.

For example, if you're in your teens or twenties and you just want to have fun, then you may not need to wait, just keep advancing as mentioned previously until she gives you a firm stop, then put the brakes on and take it a little slower.

This should go without saying but always honor her wishes, stop when she says stop and never force any advance Kino or otherwise.

On the flip side, if you want a long-term relationship and you feel this gal could be it, then you'll want to take some time to get to know her and build tension.

The reason for this is simple - men pursue sex and women pursue love and romance. Furthermore, most men will often use love to get sex and many women will use sex to get love.

Sadly, many men think that once you have sex she'll be invested and stick around for the long haul. In reality, if you haven't gotten the confidence piece down and you don't show signs of stability, she may just write you off as a fun fling.

So here's a really Big Tip, are you listening?

If you can get her to invest in you without sex, then you have a way better chance at keeping her around long-term.

When sex happens too early, the tension built is lost and both the guy and gal lose interest. Before you know it, the relationship is over.

This is why you need to build tension and more importantly, get clear on your values since this is a classic example violating values to fulfill your needs.

The value, in this case, is a long-term, committed and stable relationship but the need is intimacy. More often than not, our needs take precedence over our values because of those addictive chemicals of infatuation we mentioned earlier. When this happens, we end up in a vicious cycle of violating our values to fulfill our needs, which never gets us what we really want.

"When a guy tells me he wants to have sex it's a letdown, I feel like he doesn't know what he's doing and needs to ask me to guide him."
– Dawn

Be The Man And Lead

Remember that as the alpha, you're the leader and when it comes to sex, for the most part, you'll need to lead. While it's nice to have an aggressive woman and there's nothing wrong with that, if you tell a woman you want to sleep with her, its as if you're asking for permission.

Unfortunately, by doing this you surrender your power to her and it makes you look like every other needy guy.

Instead, make her feel like it doesn't matter if you have sex or not. And when it does come time to actually have sex, instead of asking you simply advance using the 7 steps of Kino. If she pulls back, you simply put the breaks on.

Continue Building Tension

Make sure you use the strategies in this book to continue building tension until she's practically begging for it. This is an important investment strategy, which builds love, excitement and commitment.

If you can do this, she'll respect you more because you're a challenge, you're not easy, and a challenge for most girls (especially the hot ones) is worth waiting for.

For example, if you honor your values and hold off on that intimacy (your needs or neediness) and date her for 2-3 months while building a relationship, you'll be building both trust and tension every day. Over this time she will reveal signs that may raise a red flag.

If you're already having sex, chances are you'll be hypnotized by the chemicals of infatuation and stay in the relationship just to get love (remember we think we will die if we don't get love).

So make absolutely sure you get really clear what your red flags are and make sure you have written down your values as mentioned in the **Clarity Chapter.**

"Holding out until you know its right is the difference between being a man and being a needy little boy who needs instant gratification." - Roxanne

Naturally, instant gratification without using your wisdom also leads to unwanted kids and blowing it on the biggest prize in life - your ideal match.

Quality women want a man who can resist temptation and be loyal. When you hold off and show patience, you show her you are mentally strong and won't cheat on her later on.

It also shows she is special, not just another notch in the bed, but a diamond in the rough, someone special who is worth waiting for. When she feels special (remember women want love and romance) then she'll give you the keys to her kingdom.

Tension and release

We've talked a lot about tension and when it comes to sex if you can hold off on dipping the big dipper and instead tease her, kiss her, lick her and play with you'll build mountains of tension. And the more tension you build the bigger the payoff you'll receive.

That payoff will not only be in the form of a monstrous orgasm but several other unexpected benefits like:

- She'll appreciate and respect you as a strong man with strong will power.
- She will consider you for a long-term relationship.
- You will respect her and appreciate her more than those one-night-standers.

Remember this concept and practice it, as it will serve you for the rest of your life!

Next, it's also important to understand that you don't need to get physical to make her actually feel like she's been kissed or made love to. While this may seem far fetched, we already proved the power of imagination in the study which showed how muscle could be built without actually working out.

The same is true for getting physical. If you can get a woman to start imagining things that turn her on, she will get just as hot and bothered as if she was already having fully committed sex with you.

Be careful though, if you can get to this point, she might just rip your clothes off and suck the chrome off your car bumper. Kidding aside, make sure you stimulate her imagination with sexual innuendo!

How To Move Her From Date to Your Home

After you've gone on a couple dates, you'll want to advance by bringing her home.

Sometimes women can be reluctant to make this move and will question with comments like, "Where are we going" or "What are we doing." The following are responses with sexual innuendo that use intrigue, unpredictability and false disqualifiers:

- You can only come in if you promise not to jump me.

- You can only come if you can behave yourself.

- You can only come if you promise not to laugh.

- We're just gonna stop at my place for a couple of seconds.

- I have to show you a video of this soft and furry kitten.

- You won't believe the view from my balcony; it's breathtaking.

- You can come, but only for a little bit. I turn into a pumpkin at 11

Remember to lead her and keep advancing, you'll only need to pull back if she puts the breaks on.

If for some reason she does put the break on use humor. For example, "Listen I was going to read your palm and tell you how your entire future will pan out, but it can wait."

Be Prepared or Get Shutout

Whether you come home after dinner or fix dinner for her at home, make sure you're prepared and your place is clean, with lots of sensory stimulators to get her in the mood.

This is where the men separate themselves from the boys so step it up here and follow up on this checklist:

- **Clean Sheets** – You don't want to be known as Pigpen, wash up brother!

- **Drinks In The Fridge** – While wine might be tempting, remember that its a depressant and is scientifically proven to lower libido. That being said, if she's uptight and loves wine it could come in pretty handy. Go to the store and buy some ginseng tea or hot chocolate with some actual dark chocolate on the side. Both of these are known libido increasers. Just make sure you ask her ahead of time what her beverage of choice is.

- **Sexy Music Ready To Be Played** – Music is scientifically proven to alter your mood, so take some time to investigate "sex" playlists on Spotify.

- **Candles Ready To Be Lit Or Scented Candles** – Fire resonates with the frequency of love. You'd be wasting a great opportunity if you passed on the candles. If possible get jasmine, ylang-ylang, lavender or orange blossom scented candles, which also have been proven to ignite sexual passion.

- **Infuser** – Infusers are all the rage these days and for good reason. While incense is smoky and bad for your health, an infuser can infuse powerful aromatherapy into the air. Check out some recommendations for sex scents online.

- **Condoms** – Remember, no glove no love, so get some condoms and put them next to the bed where they can be accessed without getting out of bed.

Congratulations my friend, if you've gotten to this point and **Taken** all the **Action** steps, you'll know how to approach, what to say, how to close, how to escalate and how to get her invested for the long term.

At this point, unless you blow it, you've got yourself a new girlfriend. Life doesn't get much better than spending time and sharing experiences with someone you can put your arm around and get naked with at the end of the night, so live it up my friend you deserve it!

How Not To Blow It!

In regards to that "blow it" statement, it's important you understand that just because you're dating someone, doesn't necessarily mean you'll have commitment challenges down the road.

You'll need to really work on becoming the man she's always wanted for her to stick around. More on that shortly, for now, keep in mind the process of getting a girlfriend and keeping her is a lifelong journey, so stay open to learning more from as many sources as you can. This advice alone will guarantee your success more than any other!

Chapter 11 – Putting It All Together

Eventually, if you really use the strategies from this training you'll find someone and want to date long-term or stay with them for the rest of your life.

If and when you get to this point it's important to understand that there are basically three major phases of a relationship:

1) Searching, meeting, finding the right one
2) Dating, sex, intimacy, in love
3) Loving partnership, team building

In this book, we focused primarily on step one and two but this is just the beginning of your journey. If you get to this phase and you want to keep your relationship and make it juicy long term, you'll need to learn more about dating, communication, sex, loving partnership and teambuilding.

I've had a few one-night stands, but the best sex of my life was with my boyfriend I had for 3 years. Our orgasms just kept getting better with time because we were more comfortable with each other and knew what buttons to push." -Rachel

At the end of the day, if you want to keep your new girlfriend long-term it comes down to one thing, which can be summed up in two words, can you guess what that is? Right...

Take Action!

If there is any advice I can give to help change your dating results and land the girl of your dreams, it is crucial we drill this into your head:

Take Action!

This means memorizing and using the strategies outlined in this guide to get new results.

Is There An Easier Way?

Whether you're really busy with a lot on your plate or just want a simple way to absorb this stuff, there really isn't anything easier than pressing the play button on your smartphone or stereo. Remember our Master Mantra:

Repetition Is The Mother Of All Skill?

If you simply press the play button and listen to the audio version of this training (in your car, at home, walking, etc), by listening over and over, you will by default, absorb and memorize this stuff.

Once this happens you won't have to fumble for words or guess what to do next.

But the real beauty of this strategy is that it doesn't just apply in learning how to get a girlfriend.

By listening to audiobooks, you can boost your game for anything from making more money to boosting your testosterone to learning how to be funny with relative ease.

Get This Book On Audio For FREE

Yes, you read that correctly, you can get the extended audio version of this training absolutely FREE! This contains two more chapters on advanced Kino and keeping her committed for the long-term.

All you need to do is sign up for a Free 30 day Trial on Audible, at which point you can cancel and keep the auidobook with no charge or you can continue getting two books a month for $14,95.

I personally use this service to absorb two books a month, which has boosted my life in all directions including better health, more wealth and more loving relationships.

So if you don't already own the extended Audio Version click the link below or type in the second link in your browser for a Free Audio Version of "How To Get A Girlfriend – The Ultimate Guide" on Amazon:

How to Get A Girlfriend – Audio For FREE

Or just follow this link for a FREE Version:

http://www.ChadScottCoaching.com/free-audio

Chapter 12 – Advanced Strategies

Sadly, statistics show most relationships fail to go the distance.

In the beginning, all relationships are held together by the glue of NEW. You may have experienced this as lots of excitement and sex, romance and chemical dependency.

Unfortunately, as mentioned earlier, after around two or three years this stuff starts to wear off. And if you haven't aligned your values with your partner, chances are you'll be looking for someone else within a few years.

"If a guy doesn't have his shit together, the infatuation wears down to a slow grind and eventually we start arguing. At that point, it's only a matter of time before the relationship is over." Jaden

Contrary to popular belief, finding the right person and developing a great relationship is not something that happens naturally without education. How do I know this to be true? All you have to do is look at the divorce rate.

Divorce Facts

We mentioned divorce rates at the beginning of this book but it's worth revisiting so you don't fall into this painful trap.

According to the U.S. Census Bureau, first time divorce rates for first time marriages have been dropping since 1996 but have leveled off to a shocking 41%.

But it gets worse, as the divorce rate is 60% for 2nd time marriages and 73% for 3rd time marriages.

Let's ponder this for a short second. For first time marriages, that's 4 out of every 10 marriages that will end in divorce. Now imagine 10 people you know. At some point in their lives, 4 out of those 10 will be divorced. This is not just a problem; it's a crisis, which creates an overflow of tears, heartbreak, stress, illness and pain, perhaps more than any other pain in life.

Don't Depend On Your Relationship For Your Happiness

Relationships are like rollercoasters, constantly up and down. If you rely on it as your main form of happiness, your life will be an emotional rollercoaster with constant disappointment.

Instead, focus on developing yourself, your passions and hobbies and how you can make a greater contribution to your friends, family, community and the world at large.

By developing and growing as a human being and overcoming challenges, you will develop what we call "independent" happiness, which doesn't change when you don't have money or your woman doesn't approve of you. And... women love guys who love themselves!

Now that you've read this book, you've more than likely learned some new distinctions that will help you get clear about your values, build your attraction and get that girl you've had your eye on.

For most guys, this will be the end of the road but for the guys that really are committed to lifelong learning and not only getting the girl of your dreams but also keeping her, I'd like to offer you some advanced training (Free and Paid) to really step your game up to the next level.

If you're at all hesitant to invest in yourself, I'd like to remind you that neither will she.

In other words, if you don't believe you're worth investing in, why would she invest her time in you? As so clearly stated by Billionaire Warren Buffet:

"The most important investment you can make is in yourself."

Now that we got that out of the way, I'd like to offer you some of the most powerful ways to invest in yourself.

No matter what your budget is or where you come from I have a solution that will help you become a superior man whom women from all over the world want to be with.

Get More Confidence

Let's start with the #1 attraction factor for women, which as you recall is "Confidence!

This is what separates the men from the boys and "The Natural" from the guy who has to remember pickup lines.

If you don't have much confidence, no matter how many books you read or strategies you remember, your chances of landing a high quality girlfriend are slim.

To get more confidence I recommend starting with the master guide of confidence: Get High On Confidence, which you can get for **FREE** today. Just keep reading and I'll show you how.

The Superior Man System

If you struggle with limiting beliefs about yourself like I'm not good enough, tall enough, smart enough or rich enough, you should know that with the right coach and training program these can all be changed. To make this happen I offer two options as follows:

The Winner's Mindset Training

The first option is called The Winner's Mindset, which shows you how to embed the mindsets of over 175 of the most successful people in history as your own.

This includes top artists, athletes, entrepreneurs, scientists, world leaders and sages from throughout history.

Essentially, the program will allow you to completely rewire your brain to believe you have the power and ability to not only attract beautiful women but speak to them and keep them interested long term… without any pickup lines!

But perhaps even more important is the fact that guys who have used this training have stopped failing and started winning in all areas of life including their ability to make loads of money, swaying people's opinions, and cutting the chains of fear to live a life completely free of regrets. To learn more just visit us on the web at: www.ChadScottCoaching.com

Group Coaching

The second option also includes The Winner's Mindset training but adds in a coaching element to guide you and keep you accountable long-term.

Let's face it; it takes time to rewire your brain and big changes simply don't happen overnight. What happens when you lose motivation or you get stuck three to six months down the road?

Can you imagine if you had a great coach guiding you through the minefields of past failures and encouraging you to keep on going even in the most difficult of times how much success you could've achieved?

Well, guess what? It's never too late my friend and now's the time to kick it up a few notches and get your own coach.

Because coaching is so invaluable, I offer a more affordable group coaching program as well as one-on-one coaching, both of which come with the Winner's Mindset and have completely transformed the lives of hundreds of men. To find out more visit us online at: www.ChadScottCoaching.com

Claim Your Bonuses

As promised, I've included a link to a free 90-minute video training on confidence from the Winner's Mindset. Just register your email at the link below and you'll be sent instructions on how to claim your bonus.

Free 90 Minute Confidence Training

Or follow this link:

www.ChadScottCoaching.com/winners-mindset

Get One Of Two Books For FREE

Quite simply, by taking 60 seconds to leave a review of this book on Amazon I will send you a free download of either "Online Dating - The Quick Notes" Or Get High On Confidence."

Activate Your Super Hero Power

I sell these books for just under $15 all day long on Amazon, so why would I give them away?

To be absolutely clear, my primary goal is way beyond just selling more books. The real payoff for me is to help as many people as possible rise up above rejection, insecurity and powerlessness to make their dreams a reality.

Nothing feels better than when I get an email from a reader who tells me how they used the tools in my books and trainings to break through really serious challenges and find their dream girl.

This is what gets me out of bed in the morning and why I'm giving you a FREE Book.

I Want You To Win!

By leaving a review, you not only help further your own education but you'll help other guys, which makes you a hero! This is how word spreads and more people get the help they need – simple reviews.

How To Leave A Review

- Visit the following link: https://chadscottcoaching.com/htgg and you'll be automatically redirected to the book, then scroll down until you see "Write a customer review." Make sure you're logged in or it won't be a verified review.

    Or

- Go to www.Amazon.com and search for "How To Get A Girlfriend – The Ultimate Guide by Chad Scott" click on the book, then scroll down until you see "Write a customer review." Make sure you're logged in or it won't be a verified review.

Send Me An Email with A Screenshot

After you leave a quick REVIEW about what you learned along with any suggestions for future improvement, hit the "SUBMIT" button and "TAKE A SCREENSHOT." Then send me the screenshot plus the NAME OF THE BOOK YOU WANT to:

Chad@ChadScottCoaching.com.

When I get your email I'll send you the download. It's that simple and only takes two minutes.

Remember, take action and never give up! I wish you the best on your journey and hope to see you in a future training.

Sincerely, Chad Scott

---

[i] Sherman, G. D., Lerner, J. S., Josephs, R. A., Renshon, J., & Gross, J. J. (2016). The interaction of testosterone and cortisol is associated with attained status in male executives. *Journal of Personality and Social Psychology, 110*(6), 921-929. doi.10.1037/pspp0000063

Made in the USA
Monee, IL
14 August 2021